The Pattern and the Promise

A Story of Deliverance and the Promise It Holds

HARRIET ALLEN

KINGDOM COPY PUBLISHING
400 HARRIS AVE.
PROVIDENCE, RI, 02904

ISBN 979-8-9934073-1-9

The events and details described herein are true and correct to the best knowledge and remembrance of the author. The names and details of many individuals have been changed to protect anonymity.

The butterfly emerges from its cocoon. It doesn't know what it looks like or what it's supposed to do. It doesn't see itself as the beautiful creature that God sees. It flutters about trying to find its way. Before this new life, it was a lowly worm crawling along in a limited space. Now, it's a beautiful creature flying about with unlimited freedom. Previously, it would chew on leaves and spin a web-like cocoon. Now, it sips on nectar after it breaks free from its hard shell. I am like that butterfly—a new creation in Christ. I don't yet know how beautiful I am, where I am going, or what I am going to do. But God knows, and in that I can rest.

Contents

Acknowledgements

I would like to acknowledge and thank everyone who has helped me mature and grow into the person that I am today. I also want to thank all those who helped me complete this work that the Lord assigned to me. These include so many, but particularly the following:

- My pastors in Virginia who shepherded me through my early years of growing in Christ and taught me the basics of being a new believer;
- My friends, who hosted and led a home group for many years and poured love, hospitality, friendship, and prayers into me and others to help us grow in Christ;
- My first mentor for her wisdom and guidance in leading me through my most difficult years as a new believer;
- My current pastors for their leadership and dedication to the truth of God's Word and for teaching me about the victory that we have in Christ;
- All those who reviewed this book and provided valuable feedback, while encouraging me to finish writing it;
- My children and family for bearing with me through all the years of my newfound faith and sometimes taking the blows that came with that; and
- The LORD God Almighty for rescuing me, saving me, turning my life around, and transforming it into something precious in His sight!

Introduction

Sunset Terrace is the name of the street I lived on when I first began writing this story. The name was significant to me in a couple of ways. First, it was the street I lived on as I entered the sunset years of my life. Second, it was symbolic of my view as I looked back on my life and reflected upon it.

The view from the back deck was my inspiration. I could see for miles down the Route 7 corridor in Northern Virginia—through Ashburn, Sterling, Herndon, and beyond, where this story began. Hundreds of rooftops, houses, buildings, and trees were visible at a distance, and hundreds of lights sparkled at night when the sun went down. I likened this to the view I had of my own life as I looked back and reflected on the experiences I had faced, the things I had done, and the lessons I had learned. It was like looking at a myriad of highlights in my life.

At age 47, this story began. Little did I know that it would be a time of rebirth in my life. My state of being at the time was what one could accurately call "death." There was no joy in my life, no hope, no love, and no knowledge of anything beyond darkness, hopelessness, and despair. There was no "life" left in my body either, except the thought that maybe it would be better to end it than to continue living.

I was in an extreme state of "un-wellbeing." An intense curtain of darkness and pain covered my entire being. Thoughts began to take root that maybe it *would* be better to end my life rather than to go on enduring one that hurt so much. Or maybe—a worse thought occurred to me—it might be even better to end the lives of those around me who seemed to hurt me so much. A deep, dark abyss loomed before me—a chasm so deep and dark that it could have been a bottomless black hole. There was no way to cross it or to avoid it. There was not even a bridge upon which I could cautiously inch my way across. I could only fall forward into it, not knowing where the bottom or end would be.

A journal entry I made at the time attempted to capture my thoughts:

On a path to nowhere, I sit meditating, wondering—where am I going and where have I been? Have I made the right choices? Have I done the right things? I don't know… I just don't know. Where is love? Where is appreciation? The pain in me goes deep—deep into my soul, and it burns like a slow flame. There is never a let up; it is always there—slowly simmering, rearing its ugly head to reveal its visage lest I forget it is there. Pain go away… pain, go away….

I was in a very bad place, and I didn't know what to do about it. Everything made me unhappy—my marriage, my husband, my children, my home, my career (or lack thereof), and, most of all, my thoughts about my life. I thought about how painful and unsuccessful my life had been. I thought about all of the losses I had suffered. I thought about the nagging feeling that I had to be responsible for everything. And I thought about not knowing what life was about or what I wanted to do with mine. I was angry and depressed and, frankly, I wanted an exit. I didn't have the things that I wanted to have, I couldn't be the person I wanted to be, and I couldn't accomplish what I wanted to accomplish. I might as well have been DEAD!

There were times in my life when the pain wasn't there—a birthday cake shaped like a doll's dress with a real doll in the middle when I was five years old, my cousin's wedding where I scattered rose petals as a flower girl, summer vacations to my grandmother's house in Alabama, and summer adventures with my best friend who lived down the street. Those were times of joy that I could remember. Then there was the time when my first husband and I were young and in love. Nothing could have made me happier.

One other thing brought peace and solace into my life. As a child, I spent time in the woods by myself—close to nature, empowered and energized by the simple beauty of a gently trickling stream of water, a cool breeze ruffling through the trees, and the perfect harmony of God's creatures all around me.

SEARCHING FOR ANSWERS

I spent most of my adult life searching for some kind of meaning and fulfillment. Why had I suffered so many heartaches? Why did I have an alcoholic father who would go on violent rages and threaten to kill my mother with a butcher knife in the middle of the night? Why did I have a critical, controlling mother who, though well-intentioned, constantly criticized me and beat me with a wooden paddle whenever I made a mistake? Why did I have to care for younger siblings all the time—screaming and fighting with them to maintain some kind of control? And why did I have to lie to bill collectors on the phone while my parents stood by and coached me?

Why did the love of my life have to die at the age of 35? Why was my life so unsuccessful and unproductive? I wanted to be a teacher, but grew disillusioned by the students' unruly behavior. Why was I fired from an editing job four months after my husband died? I searched for years to find what would make me happy and fulfilled, but I was unable to find it.

Then, when I was 47 years old, something took hold of me and changed my life. I didn't ask for God's intervention in my life. However, unaware of His existence, I had cried out to Him for about a year because of the pain and heartache I was experiencing. With the advent of Christmas that year and a neighbor's tragic suicide after that, circumstances brought me back to a place I never dreamed I'd be. I attended a friend's church to find out what my eldest son was up to, and rivers of grief and regret poured out of me for about a year. Several subsequent supernatural events convinced me that God truly exists, and that He is an all-powerful, all-knowing, and all-present being.

This is a story I can't defend; I can only say it is real, and I experienced it. Some of the things I will share I'm not proud of. In fact, they are things I am ashamed of because they were foolish, though I thought they were right at the time. This isn't an excuse; it's simply an observation. If it weren't for the intervention of a wonderful heavenly Father, who loves me more than I ever could have imagined, I would still be stuck in the same sad, fatalistic mindset. It would only have kept leading me down a spiraling path of pain, anger, and hopelessness.

This story of God's pattern for deliverance and restoration is told as I experienced it in my life. I want people to know that God is real, that He loves each and every one of us more than we can imagine, and that He desires a personal relationship with us. I want people to know that this life is not all there is to existence. It really is a place for us to choose whether or not we want to be reconciled to God, our Father, with protection, provision, purpose, and a place for us. I want people to know that, although God is Spirit and not someone we can readily see, feel, or touch in the natural sense, He is completely revealed through the One He calls His Son, Jesus Christ. We can experience Him in the realm of the Spirit, as well as in the fellowship of His Word and with other believers.

One of my early journal entries describes what ultimately took me many years to internalize and what I am still in the process of learning:

When you reach a point of desperation, where nothing else matters, where you feel willing to die for someone or something, that is the point where God wants you to come to the cross. God wants you to realize that He loves you and the rest of the world so much that nothing else matters. He laid down the life of his only Son, Jesus Christ, to save all of mankind from destruction.

God wants you to realize His love for you so that you can love and forgive yourself, love and forgive one another, and ultimately, live in peace and harmony, reunited with Him. You have to accept the fact that you are not perfect and that others are not perfect. You have to love God and His Son, Jesus, so much that you are willing to lay down your 'fleshly' life for Him and live according to His will. You have to learn to trust that He will provide for your every need. He can provide the love and comfort you need if you trust in Him. He can provide the truth and answers you need if you trust in Him. He can provide a way through your problems and give you a meaningful life if you trust in Him.

As I recount my journey of deliverance along God's road of redemption, I hope this story will help you navigate similar circumstances that you may encounter and give you the courage to persevere. I also hope that this story will encourage anyone who, at one time or another, may have given their lives to the Lord Jesus Christ but has since given up on their walk with God. If that is you, my hope is that you will return to the Lord and continue your journey until you experience the goodness of God *"in the land of the living"* (Psalm 27:13).

CHAPTER 1
December 17 – the Blood

"Tell the whole community of Israel that on the tenth day of this month each man is to take a lamb for his family, one for each household…. Then they are to take some of the blood and put it on the sides and tops of the doorframes of the houses where they eat the lambs…. The blood will be a sign for you on the houses where you are; and when I see the blood, I will pass over you. No destructive plague will touch you when I strike Egypt."

EXODUS 12:3, 7, 13

December 17—a fairly warm and balmy day for a week before Christmas in Northern Virginia. I had just returned from visiting a local new-age shop, hoping to find a few unique Christmas gifts for my family. Instead, I came home with a couple of new Christmas CDs for myself. Our three-story townhouse sat on the inside corner of a group of seven townhomes forming a U-shape around an oval parking lot. Our end unit was situated at the back corner of the "U." The paved parking lot and small front yards were lined with mature trees. A row of angled parking spaces lined one side of an island in the center of the "U," which was bordered by a hedge and large pine trees.

As I sat down on the sofa in my living room to relax and listen to one of my new CDs, a police officer suddenly burst through the front door and stood in the foyer. In an instant, I found myself looking down the hallway from my living room, gawking at a large, bulky, uniformed man standing just inside my front door.

"Where is he?" he demanded, hurried and anxious.

"What?" I replied, still looking incredulously at the officer standing in my foyer and trying to process the fact that an officer of the law had just burst into my home.

"Oh, I must have the wrong house," he said and quickly exited through the front door almost as suddenly as he had entered.

'What the h…. is going on?' I thought to myself. Curiosity consumed me, and I followed him outside to see what had brought him to my neighborhood. Immediately,

I was met by an extremely unsettling scene. Two police cars, with lights flashing, lined the curb in front of my neighbor's house, directly to the right of ours. My neighbor, Diane, was standing in the parking lot in front of her house, talking with the police. Her children were sitting in their van parked alongside the curb next to her. Curious neighbors were starting to gather around. My gaze lingered on her children, and I saw a look of frightened panic on their faces. I summoned as much courage as I could to walk over to Diane and ask her what happened.

"David shot himself," she said. "We had an argument, and I left the house. When I came back, I found him upstairs in the bathroom next to our bedroom."

"Did the kids see him?" I asked.

"No. They were with me, but they stayed in the car. We were going to stay over at my sister's house. When I came back to get something, I went into the house, and that's when I found him."

David was Diane's husband. They had been living next to us for several years, but I didn't know them very well. I knew that she was a stay-at-home mom, that they were Christians, and that they home-schooled their kids. As I stood there talking with her, I looked at David Jr., who was sitting in the front seat of the van, staring blankly through the window at the scene on the street. David Jr. was about 14, the middle of the three children, and the oldest son. He sat there frozen, motionless, eyes wide open, looking like a deer in the headlights of a car, seemingly trying to process whatever his young teenage brain could about the situation. Their daughter, Dora, about 16, and their youngest son, Daniel, about 8, were sitting in the back seat of the van, staring with equal terror and apprehension.

I walked up to the van. "Everything's going to be alright," I told David Jr., trying to reassure him, yet unsure of how things would turn out. I then looked at the other children. "Everything's going to be alright," I repeated, trying to reassure them as well.

"Is there some place we can talk?" the police officer asked Diane. I invited them to come into my house. By that time, another neighbor and mutual friend of ours, Sharlene, had arrived on the scene. She accompanied us into my house, and we sat with Diane on the sofa while the officer talked with her.

"This was a very selfish act," the officer began. I looked quizzically at him, and he must have noticed my expression. "For someone who has a wife and three children and is the only breadwinner in the family, it is a very selfish act to take one's life and leave the family without any means of support," he explained.

The family had been facing problems for a while. Diane informed us that David had been job-hopping for the past year and was currently unemployed. He had held several positions, but couldn't keep them because he argued with his managers. Diane also mentioned that David was on medication for depression. After this incident, Diane was now left with three children, no insurance, and no means of support. 'This truly was a selfish act,' I thought to myself.

Into the Scene of the "Crime"

After the police removed the body and Diane left with the kids to go to her sister's house, Sharlene and I went into the house to help clean up the mess. The place looked like a cyclone had torn through it. Empty drawers and clothes cascaded down the front stairs as we entered the foyer. It looked as if someone had just flung everything down the stairs in a torrent of rage. We went to the back of the house and entered the kitchen. Dirty pans of stale food lay on the stove and in the sink. A row of prescription bottles of various sizes and shapes lined the back of the counter. 'Yes,' I thought to myself, looking at the bottles, 'David definitely must have been depressed and was taking a lot of meds for it.'

Sharlene and I exchanged surprised looks. "Where should we start?" I asked.

"I'll clean the bathroom if you want to clean the kitchen and stairs," Sharlene said.

"Sure," I replied.

She gathered a couple of buckets and some cleaning supplies from a closet and started up the stairs to find the bathroom. I started picking up all the debris on the front stairway and put it back into the drawers. Then I went into the kitchen and cleaned the dirty pots and pans. After I finished, I went upstairs to help Sharlene.

"My god, what happened?" I said, rather startled at the scene that lay before me as I stood in the doorway to the master bathroom. A large pool of thickened, congealed blood surrounded the base of the toilet, and more covered the bottom of the bathtub. Sharlene was leaning over the tub, gingerly coaxing the congealed blood down the drain, a little at a time.

"David shot himself in the head," Sharlene replied. "It appears he was rather thoughtful about it too—he leaned over the bathtub so it would catch most of the blood. The bullet hole is in the wall next to you," she continued.

"Oh, I see," I said, turning and staring at the bullet hole next to me, still somewhat in disbelief and trying to process something I had never seen before in my life.

"I'll start on the floor around the toilet," I responded bravely, looking at the pool of congealed blood on the floor around the toilet and thinking I could knock this job out in no time at all.

I wet my sponge and began to mop up the blood around the toilet. It was so thick and red and gooey that it took several attempts just to make a slight depression in it. As I mopped, I began feeling sicker and sicker. A growing sense that this pool of blood would take forever to clean up and the realization that a human life had just perished there began to take hold of me. Slowly, the enormity of the situation and the reality of what had occurred unexpectedly and forcefully overwhelmed me.

"I'm not sure I can do this," I said to Sharlene after a little while. "I'm getting sick to my stomach."

"It's OK," she replied. "I'll do it."

"Are you sure?" I didn't want to leave her with such a messy job to do all alone, but I knew I was struggling to handle it and was feeling sicker and sicker, to the point where I thought I might vomit and make things even worse.

"Yes," she assured me. "I'm used to seeing blood. I've cleaned up a few bloody messes in my life."

I didn't ask what she meant or how she could do it so nonchalantly, but I agreed to leave the job and go straighten up the rest of the house while she cleaned the bathroom. After we both finished, we left the house and went our separate ways.

The Pattern Begins

A few days later, I was invited to Diane's house to meet her family. I decided to go and offer my condolences. A few family members were sitting in a circle in the living room when I arrived.

"I'm very sorry for your loss," I told them, standing and quietly surveying the group.

"We're very thankful for your friendship with Diane and for your help in cleaning up," someone said.

"I was only doing what I thought I was supposed to do," I replied.

"We knew it," someone said. "You're an angel." At that, everyone laughed.

"No, I'm not an angel," I replied. "I was only doing what I thought I was supposed to do," I repeated. Then we chatted and visited for a little while.

Returning home, I thought about what that person had said about my being an angel. 'No, I'm definitely not an angel,' I thought to myself. But something had changed in me. I was beginning to sense something eerie and strange that I really couldn't describe—something unnatural that existed unseen beyond myself and the world around me.

A few days later, I was still thinking about the entire incident, replaying everything that happened in my mind. The image of the blood and the loss of a human life kept lingering and haunting me. I couldn't get it out of my head. Suddenly, a thought hit me: *"Jesus shed his blood for me, and it looked just like* the *blood I saw that day in the bathroom!"* Everything I had been taught more than 20 years earlier about Jesus' shedding his blood for me and His death on the cross came flooding back, and the enormity of the event shocked me. 'Wow,' I thought, 'I never realized how much that sacrifice really meant—until now.'

A few years later, when I began reading the Bible, I was reflecting on this event and noticed a connection between what I was reading and what was happening in my own life. I saw a parallel between the lamb's blood that was spread on the doorframes of the Israelites' houses, protecting them from the death angel, and Jesus' blood shed on the cross to save me from eternal death. It marked the start of God's pattern of deliverance that He revealed to me as I read through the Bible in those early years.

The Pattern

THE COVENANT OF BLOOD

The blood of a perfect lamb spread on the doorframes
of the Israelites' houses protected them from the Angel
of Death that passed over Egypt on the night of God's
final judgment against Pharaoh.

The blood of Jesus, God's perfect Lamb, protects us
from eternal death when we repent and accept His
sacrifice for our sins.

CHAPTER 2
Out of Captivity

During the night Pharaoh summoned Moses and Aaron and said, "Up!
Leave my people, you and the Israelites! Go, worship the LORD as you
have requested".... So the people took their dough before the yeast was
added, and carried it on their shoulders in kneading troughs wrapped in
clothing.... And on that very day the LORD brought the Israelites out of
Egypt by their divisions.

EXODUS 12:31, 34, 51

A couple of weeks after David's suicide, I was staring out my kitchen window at a broken table on top of the trash pile at the end of my driveway. Its glory days, when it had rested stately in the splendor of a custom-decorated model home, were long over. It had been a beautiful tray table—octagonal in shape, made of dark mahogany wood with turned-up edges all around and a center medallion inset of lightly colored wood. Its four pairs of gracefully turned legs were joined underneath by crisscrossing bars, each with an Oriental-inspired design where they met, giving the overall appearance of an artistic piece of Oriental handiwork.

My mother had given me the table from one of my stepfather's model homes, and now I was looking at it sitting on the trash pile in front of my house—forsaken, forlorn, and broken—an abused and rejected pile of wood that had lost its usefulness and beauty. It was now just a scrap of debris teetering on top of a heap of garbage bags. Its Oriental legs were broken and splintered; the joining bars that supported and connected them were missing a piece that now lay beside them on the garbage heap. The top was scratched and trampled, having been thoroughly jumped on, climbed on, and beaten upon by our three boys. It once was a treasured piece of art; now it was a useless piece of rubbish.

In a way, it had embodied all the hopes and dreams I had envisioned for my life. Now, it lay broken by three young, rambunctious boys. What was left of it was held together only by the limited energy I could muster each day to manage the boys' behavior. The table was broken, my family was broken, my marriage was broken, and my life was broken. I had little hope that the dreams of a happy marriage and family would ever come to pass. Little did I know that I would see that table again in the not-too-distant future.

I had three sons in my life at that time—a 16-year-old, an 8-year-old, and a 6-year-old. The 16-year-old had just begun attending church with Sharlene's daughter. I had been active in church as a teenager, singing in the choir and taking part in Sunday youth group. While I enjoyed the youth group activities and the Sunday dinners the group hosted to raise money, I didn't have a positive experience with church in general during those years.

First, there was the question about Adam and Eve that my pastor couldn't answer to my satisfaction—where did their wives come from? "It was symbolic," he said. 'Really? How do you have children with a symbolic wife?' I thought. Second, there was the pastor's son whom I dated once and didn't think I was going to make it home with all of my clothes on. Third, there was the lady who sat next to me in the pew one Sunday who told me if I didn't stop cracking my chewing gum, she would "crack" me—not to mention the boring liturgies and interminable, irrelevant sermons that we had to endure.

My most negative church experience, however, happened one summer in my late teens as I was preparing to start college. I had gone to an outdoor craft fair and stopped at a booth to look over some handmade jewelry and scarves. A small, petite woman, rather plainly dressed, quietly stood and watched me peruse the table.

"Do you believe in Jesus?" she suddenly asked.

"Yes," I replied, somewhat hesitantly, surprised that she would ask such a personal question. But I continued to browse through the scarves and jewelry.

"Are you sure?" she asked again, this time in a more demanding voice.

"Yes, I'm sure," I replied, growing impatient with her repeated questioning. I had been baptized at age 16 in my church, and I was pretty confident that I believed in Jesus and was saved.

"How do you know for sure?" she continued to press.

"I just know," I replied, disgusted by her persistent, invasive questioning, and I walked away.

'How dare she question my belief in Jesus and my salvation?' I thought to myself. 'That is really a personal thing, and I don't even know her.' Her questioning had invaded my sense of personal space; it made me angry, and I didn't like it. 'With people like her in the faith,' I thought, 'I don't ever want to go back to church.'

Consequently, still feeling skeptical and angry about that experience, I was hesitant to return to church after my neighbor's suicide. However, I decided I needed to go and see what my 16-year-old son was up to, as he was attending church regularly with Sharlene's daughter. Besides, there was the revelation about Jesus and his blood that I had experienced, and I was curious to explore that further. So, two weeks after David committed suicide, I arrived at church, alongside my 16-year-old son, for the first time in 28 years since the incident at the craft fair—which happened to be New Year's Eve.

A New View of Church

Coming into the church, I was quite surprised at the change that had taken place since I had last attended church. The congregation was meeting in a large room of an office building. In the "sanctuary," there were rows of chairs arranged in a V-shape. At the front, there was a small table set up as an altar and a slightly raised platform to the right with a three-piece band on it.

My neighbor, Sharlene, unknown to me, happened to be singing with the band up front that day. Her voice was so sweet and melodious that she sounded like an angel. I was both surprised and stunned—I never knew she had such talent! Somehow, I hadn't put it together in my mind that she attended the same church as her daughter. Listening to her sing released a flood of emotions in me, causing the past 28 years of pain, anger, loss, and failure to surface and pour out in a torrent of tears. This continued almost every week for nearly a year as I kept returning to the church every Sunday with my son.

After church that first day, one of the women came up to me and invited me to a New Year's Eve party at her house that night. She also asked me if I'd like to meet the pastor.

"Yes," I said. She escorted me into a small office off the sanctuary and introduced me to the pastor. After some brief introductions, he asked me if I had any questions.

"Yes," I said. "It's something I've been thinking about... If Jesus is the only way to be saved, what about all the other religions around the world and the people who believe in them? What will happen to them if they don't believe in Jesus? Will they be saved?"

"I suggest you pray about that," he replied. It sounded like such a trite answer, but he also seemed so calm and confident about it that I decided to follow his advice. So, on the way home, I did just that.

"Nothing Matters But My Son"

The next day was New Year's Day. Traditionally, I like to prepare a pork roast for New Year's dinner, served with mashed potatoes, sauerkraut (even though I was the only one in the family who liked it), and black-eyed peas. My mother, who grew up in the South, always said that pork and black-eyed peas were traditional Southern New Year's dishes believed to bring good luck. I couldn't argue with that—I liked the idea of starting the New Year with good luck.

I had enjoyed a good time the night before at my new friend Kelly's New Year's Eve party, so I got a late start on dinner the next day. I put the pork roast in the oven early in the afternoon and was about to start peeling the potatoes when, suddenly, I had a vague recollection that I had heard my 16-year-old son go out the front door some time ago, and he hadn't come back. That was unusual for him—leaving the house on a holiday. He also had seemed unusually depressed lately. I didn't know why, but with his being such a sensitive person and his leaving and not coming back yet, as well as David's suicide still fresh in my mind, I began to worry that something might have happened to him.

'What should I do?' I thought. 'I'm in the middle of fixing our traditional New Year's dinner, but my son has left the house, seeming very depressed lately, and he hasn't come back yet. Should I continue fixing dinner and wait longer to see if he comes back, or should I go out and look for him?' By this time, I was getting really worried about him. 'Nothing matters but my son,' I thought. Consequently, I decided to abandon the New Year's dinner temporarily and go out to look for him.

I hopped into my car and started driving around the neighborhood to see if I could find him. When I couldn't locate him, I broadened my search to nearby neighborhoods and friends' houses where I thought he might be. Throughout this, I kept thinking that my family wouldn't have a New Year's dinner and felt guilty because I was out looking for my son instead of at home preparing dinner. 'Nothing matters but my son,' I kept telling myself, torn between these conflicting thoughts. 'This is more important than anything else—to make sure he is safe and okay,' I finally determined. So, I kept searching for him.

After searching for a while, I couldn't find him. So, I went home and waited, abandoning my plans to fix New Year's dinner at that point. Eventually, he returned home, and I asked where he had been. "To the Village Center," he said. He'd been feeling a little depressed and went to the Center to think for a bit. But he was okay, he assured me, and I didn't need to worry.

As I sat on the sofa, relieved that he had come home and was okay, I reflected on what had gone through my mind that day. 'Nothing matters but my son....' I had kept thinking that phrase and repeating it to myself. Then, it hit me—God had answered my prayer! *"Nothing matters but my Son—who is Jesus!"* That was the answer to my prayer and the question I had asked the pastor the day before. I didn't understand it at the time, nor did I see how it could save everyone in the world. Still, I knew with certainty that this was God's answer to my question and my prayer, and that was good enough for me.

Thus, a new year and a new life were beginning for me. Just as the blood of a lamb saved the Israelites from the Angel of Death and brought them out of captivity, Jesus, the Lamb of God (John 1:29), was delivering me from captivity to a life of pain, loss, and disappointment. I was leaving "spiritual Egypt" behind, and God's pattern of deliverance was continuing.

The Pattern

RELEASE FROM BONDAGE

The blood of a lamb saved the Israelites from the Angel of Death and delivered them from captivity and bondage in Egypt, leading them to start a new life in God's Promised Land.

The blood of Jesus, God's perfect Lamb, delivers us from captivity to the kingdom of darkness, ruled by the god of this world, and transfers us into God's Kingdom of light, ruled by Jesus Christ, to start a new life in Him.

CHAPTER 3
Miracles

Then Moses stretched out his hand over the sea, and all that night the
LORD drove the sea back with a strong east wind and turned it into dry
land. The waters were divided, and the Israelites went through the sea on
dry ground, with a wall of water on their right and on their left.

EXODUS 14:21-22

The following week, I went back to church, then the week after that, and again the week after that. My friendship with Kelly, my new friend, also grew closer. One day, we were talking on the phone, and she shared a story about a time when her daughter Nadia was very sick. Nadia had registered a high fever and was having difficulty breathing. Kelly thought she might need to take Nadia to the hospital. She and a friend decided to lay hands on Nadia and pray. By the next morning, Nadia was feeling better, and her fever was gone.

The next day, I was walking our dog, Ginger, along a sidewalk toward our Village Center. It was a beautiful, sunny, late summer day. The air was still; there was no wind, and the atmosphere was quiet and peaceful. I was thinking about the conversation Kelly had shared with me about her daughter Nadia the night before. 'Can prayer really be that powerful?' I wondered, as Ginger and I strolled along the sidewalk in the late afternoon.

As soon as that thought crossed my mind, I heard a loud, audible *crack,* and a forty-foot-tall pine tree across the street uprooted itself and fell behind us, just missing us as we hurried up the sidewalk to get out of its way.

'Wow—that really caught my attention!' I thought. I looked around to see the tip of the tree just brushing the edge of the sidewalk behind us. Its massive trunk and branches completely blocked any chance of cars passing through on the street. A large, turned-up root ball across the street stood majestically and quietly next to the hole it had once occupied. Without any wind or other natural cause to trigger it, the strange event both surprised and convinced me that God was making a point.

"Ok, I get the message," I said to myself. "I guess prayer really is that powerful." While I said this to myself, I also directed my thoughts toward God at the same time. Thus, I started talking to Him.

As the weeks went by, more and more supernatural events unfolded in my life. One day, as I walked Ginger along a path around our neighborhood, I reflected on the magnitude of what I was learning about God and His nature. 'You truly are omnipotent, omniscient, and omnipresent,' I thought, subconsciously directing the statement to Him as I strolled beneath a canopy of maples and pines.

Once again, as soon as that thought went through my mind, a loud rustling sound rushed through the trees behind me, as if a strong breeze had blown through the leaves. But when I looked around, nothing was moving. The trees were still, the leaves weren't rustling, and the sky shone bright and sunny above us. 'Wow! God heard that one too!' I thought, surprised and excited that He had once again confirmed His existence to me.

There was another time after church one Sunday when one of my sons wanted a couple of quarters to get a soda from the soda machine. I didn't have any quarters, so I told him we had to pass on that because I didn't have enough money. On the way to our car in the parking lot, I reached into my coat pocket to get my car keys. When I pulled my keys out, two quarters flew out of my pocket at the same time, along with my keys, onto the ground in front of me. There lay the quarters that my son needed to buy his soda. I never carry change in my pocket, and I know for a fact that those quarters weren't there before that. Once again, God had revealed His miraculous nature and His existence to me.

An Angelic Experience

One of the strangest events that happened to me took place around Christmas the following year. A friend invited me to a holiday party, but I was overwhelmed with things to do and didn't feel I could go. "What is happening in my life?" I prayed on the way home one night. So many things demanded my attention, and the peace I initially felt was starting to fade quickly.

I decided to stop at the grocery store on my way home that evening to pick up a few things we needed. The store was virtually deserted. As I usually do, I placed my purse in the front section of the cart, which was designed as a child's seat. I picked up several items and placed them in my cart, then strolled over to the bulk foods section to get some oatmeal.

As I scooped up rolled oats from one of the barrels, a young man in his early 20s with curly dark hair and wearing a suit approached the bulk food barrels and stood a short distance behind my cart, looking at the barrels. Suddenly, he reached out his hand and began to pull my cart toward him. Surprised that he would so blatantly pull my cart toward him while I was standing there and worried that my purse was still sitting in the child's seat nearby, I said rather emphatically, "That's my cart!"

"I know," he replied. Then, he released the cart and casually walked toward the checkout lines at the front of the store without saying another word. Curious about who he was and why he did that, I followed him a few seconds later toward the front of the store, but he was nowhere in sight.

'That was the strangest experience,' I thought to myself. 'Who was that person, and what was that about? That young man obviously knew what he was doing. I had looked directly at him and spoken to him. He said he *knew* it was my cart, but he didn't try to steal it or my purse while I was standing there. Who was he? Could he have been an angel?'

The following Tuesday, I spoke with my pastor, Mark, about it and told him what had happened, noting that I had been overwhelmed by so many things demanding my attention lately.

"What do you think that was about?" I asked him. "Do you think he could have been an angel?"

"He probably was an angel," Mark replied. "He may have been trying to show you that Satan will try to steal what you have if you let him." Once again, it seemed God had answered my prayer, showing me what was happening in my life. So many things were demanding my attention and they were beginning to steal my peace.

There was another time when the mom of one of my middle son's friends came by our house looking for her son. He wasn't there, but I invited her in for a minute. We were standing in my front hallway, casually chatting about school, soccer, and other "moms of boys" things. We stood about 15 to 18 feet apart—she was standing at one end of the hallway near the front door, and I was at the other end near the living room.

I recently had thought about the power of God's Word, how He created the world with just His Word, and I had prayed to understand that more deeply. During our conversation, as I was speaking, one of my words suddenly and unexpectedly burst out of my mouth with a strong "whoosh," or burst of air, which I could not control. It felt as if it had a life and power of its own, carrying it from my mouth to her ears. It startled me, and I'm sure it surprised her too, because she had a look of surprise on her face. We both stood there silently for a moment, gazing incredulously at each other, saying nothing. Then, without mentioning it, we continued our conversation as if nothing had happened. But I knew once again that God had answered my prayer, and I had momentarily experienced the creative power of His Word.

A SUPERNATURAL ANOINTING

Perhaps the most significant supernatural event I experienced happened one evening during a Women's Meeting at our church. About a year earlier, one of the women in the church had asked me if I wanted to receive the "baptism of the Holy Spirit." "Yes," I said, and she prayed for me to receive it.

At the end of the Women's Meeting, a Jewish believer named Leah, who was the wife of one of the elders in the church, stood up to pray for the women seeking prayer. Eager to leave and get home because it was late, I quickly stood up and maneuvered my way to the front of the line. The other women all lined up behind me.

Leah applied some anointing oil to her fingers and then placed them on my forehead as she prepared to pray for me. The moment she put the oil on my forehead, I experienced a sudden, bright flash of light in my mind and had an instant vision of Heaven's opening up. Immediately, I lost all strength in my body, my legs weakened, and I slumped to the floor. My mouth started moving uncontrollably, and I found myself quickly and involuntarily making sounds that were completely foreign to me—all the while having no strength or control in my body to move anything, including my mouth.

This went on for several minutes as Leah prayed for the women in line behind me. During that time, the pastor's wife, Tara, cradled me in her arms while my mouth continued to move and utter uncontrollable sounds. As things started to slow down, Tara asked me what I was praying for. Somehow, I knew that the sounds I was making were prayers for others, and I had a sense of whom they were for. I extended my arm and waved my hand along the line of women waiting for prayer. "All of them," I muttered, as best I could.

On the way home that night, I could barely drive. I felt as if I were drunk, but I hadn't had anything to drink. I drove slowly and carefully, still feeling "intoxicated" from my experience and thinking about what had happened. I had witnessed a momentary vision of Heaven, and I had spoken in uncontrollable, foreign sounds. I didn't know or understand why, but I knew at that point that God had blessed me with the baptism of the Holy Spirit.

By this time, I also knew beyond a doubt that God was real and that He was an all-powerful, all-present, and all-knowing being. Just as He did with the Israelites when parting the sea for them to cross on dry ground, God had demonstrated his miracle-working power to me. All was well with my soul, and I couldn't stop seeking to know Him more.

The Pattern

CONFIRMING MIRACLES

God confirmed the reality of His existence and His
all-powerful nature to the Israelites through miracles,
signs, and wonders as they crossed the Red Sea on dry
ground and continued their journey to the Promised Land.

God proves His existence and power to us through miracles,
signs, and wonders as we accept Jesus into our
hearts and start to follow Him as our Lord and Savior.

CHAPTER 4
Into the Wilderness

In the desert the whole community grumbled against Moses and Aaron.
The Israelites said to them, "If only we had died by the LORD's hand in
Egypt! There we sat around pots of meat and ate all the food we wanted,
but you have brought us out into this desert to starve this entire assembly
to death."

EXODUS 16:2-3

At this stage in my new life with God, I started reading the Bible regularly. I had taken a class offered by the pastor for new believers. "At a minimum," he strongly recommended, "you need to read the first five books of the Bible, known as the Pentateuch, along with Proverbs, Psalms, and the New Testament. If you also can read the prophets Isaiah, Jeremiah, and Ezekiel, that would be even better."

So, I started reading, and as I read, I couldn't put it down. It took me about three years to read through the entire Bible. Certain words or phrases would jump out at me as being "truth," and others would convict me of sin. When that happened, I would repent and pray for the Lord to forgive me. As I read, I also began to see the pattern more clearly that God was revealing to me. I was experiencing situations in my own life that resembled what I was reading in the Old Testament. My life was mirroring the account of the Israelites as they journeyed to the Promised Land, and God was showing me His pattern for deliverance!

By now, I could see that I had been saved by the blood of God's perfect Lamb, Jesus, just as the Israelites were saved by the blood of a sacrificial lamb spread on the doorframes and lintels of their houses. I had been set free from slavery to the kingdom of this world and had witnessed miracles in my life, much like the Israelites were set free from slavery in Egypt and witnessed miracles in the desert as they fled Pharaoh's army.

Then, I began to go through a "wilderness" or "desert" experience. I felt cut off from the world and from those close to me. I was alone, secluded, and isolated. I no longer fit in with my family or old friends, and I also didn't fit in with my "new" family and friends—God's family. Everything felt unfamiliar and strange. I didn't know how to speak or behave around these "Christians," and I didn't understand what was happening in my life.

I was still dealing with pain, sorrow, and grief; yet I didn't know what to do about it or where to turn. I was stumbling, wandering along an unfamiliar path in a "wilderness." Like the Israelites on their journey to the Promised Land, I began to grumble and complain. I wondered why God had led me into this new life that didn't seem much better than the one I had left.

At this point, I recalled several times in my past when it seemed that God had tried to reach me, but I had shut Him out or dismissed Him. The first was during my college years. As an English major, I had been given the opportunity to take a course in the history of the Bible. Despite feeling repeatedly that I should enroll in the course, I avoided it like the plague. I was still reeling from my experience at the craft fair and wanted nothing to do with the Bible or its history.

The second time was during the years when my first husband was sick. The local Catholic church, not far from our house, had called to invite us to attend. Even though my husband was raised Catholic and we were married in a Catholic church, I still harbored suspicion of any church and refused to go there or accept their help.

A third time, our next-door neighbors, who knew my husband was sick, invited us to their home to join something called "A Course in Miracles." I was suspicious of that too and wanted nothing to do with it. Sometimes I wonder whether God would have entered my life sooner and my life might have taken a different path if I had accepted any of these invitations.

Now, however, God had made Himself unmistakably known to me, and I couldn't turn back. I began journaling and recording my thoughts and feelings as God started working in my life to change me. I was broken and scarred and felt unloved, but I also was thirsty and eager to know God more. God's Word was transforming me as I read it, and I was struggling to adapt to my new way of life (Matthew 13:20-22), but I had to keep pursuing this mysterious being.

SHARING MY TESTIMONY

During this time, I shared my "testimony" at my church's home group. The group met every Tuesday night at a member's house. We usually enjoyed dinner together, followed by our meeting. One member, Mary Rose, was an excellent cook. She prepared the meal most weeks, and we all chipped in to cover the cost, as well as helped with setting up and cleaning up. Mary Rose was an older woman in her late 60s. She became known as the "pie lady" because she baked the most delicious pies from scratch. After dinner, we all gathered in the living room for a pre-planned program, which ranged from prayer and worship to teaching or sharing. That night, I shared my testimony about my life and how I came to know the Lord.

I shared how I had been crying out to God for about a year before He intervened, not really knowing who God was or if He was real. I only knew that I was in so much pain and my life was such a mess that I didn't think I wanted to live anymore. The only thing that kept me going at that time was my children. I had been in my second marriage for about eight years, and I felt no love in the marriage. My life was consumed by a constant struggle to be a good mom, raise my kids, and teach them what I thought they needed to know.

My first husband had died at age 35 from Hodgkin's disease, a cancer we believed had been caused by his exposure to Agent Orange while serving in the Air Force. We fell in love right after high school and kept in touch during the four years he served in the military. When he was discharged, we got married and enjoyed seven happy years together before he fell ill. He was sick for five more years before he passed away. Those five years were long and grueling for both of us—not only because of his illness, but also because we had a baby to care for during the last three years of his life.

We had attempted several alternative treatments to thwart his Hodgkin's disease —all to no avail. We tried intravenous injections of laetrile, a popular and well-known alternative cancer treatment at the time. We bought a juicer and prepared organic vegetable juices daily for him to drink. We visited a doctor in New York who claimed to have successfully treated cancer patients with selenium, and we tried injections of that mixture.

In the end, nothing worked, and his cancer spread. We eventually resorted to traditional treatments of radiation and chemotherapy, but I think by then, my husband had given up. After he died, his brother, with whom he had been living the last several months of his life, found pills prescribed to strengthen his immune system hidden around his room.

I believe I also had given up, although I could never fully admit to myself that the love of my life was going to die. After five years of struggling and helping him fight his disease, I lacked the strength and energy to care for him and our three-year-old son while working full-time. As a result, he went to live with his brother in

California to help care for him. That is where he eventually died a few months later. My mother, our young son, and I arrived at the hospital the night before the doctors removed his life support, and I was able to hold his hand and say goodbye before he left this life.

MY LIFE GROWING UP

My life growing up was a struggle as well. I grew up in Ohio in a mostly dysfunctional family. I was the oldest of four children, with two younger sisters and a younger brother. I was an A/B student and a well-behaved kid. During my childhood, I helped my family through some difficult and heart-wrenching years.

Dad was an alcoholic who was gone most of the time. He managed to get various sales jobs selling products like Fuller brushes and Kirby vacuums, but he never kept them for long because of his drinking. For a while, he had a good job with one of the rubber companies in Cleveland, and we lived in a nice, middle-class neighborhood and attended good schools. However, Dad eventually would disappear again on one of his drinking binges, and Mom would find out he was in jail somewhere or carousing with another woman.

I remember feeling incredibly embarrassed, ashamed, and disappointed when I would wake up in the morning and look out my bedroom window, which faced the front of our house, only to see Dad's car parked crookedly in the middle of the street. That was a clear sign to us and the neighbors that he had been on a drinking binge and had come home drunk once again!

One night, I was awakened in the middle of the night when my mom called me for help from downstairs in the kitchen. I hurried down the stairs and froze at the kitchen door when I saw my dad at one end of the kitchen, wielding a butcher knife and threatening to kill my mother, while she stood terrified at the other end. He had been drinking, and they had been arguing.

I remember calmly but firmly telling my dad to put down the knife. I think I was about 12 years old at the time. Why he listened to a 12-year-old kid, I'll never know, but I believe that God's grace must have been at work in that situation, because he did put down the knife and subsequently left the house.

My youngest sister tells me that Dad was physically abusive to us, but I don't remember some of the stories she shares. I do remember a time when my sisters and I were in the kitchen alone with him one evening, and Dad was drunk again. He asked me to fix him some fried chicken. Being only about 14 at the time, I told him I didn't know how to make fried chicken. He kept repeating it, and I kept telling him I didn't know how to make it. Finally, he got so angry that he picked up my youngest sister and threw her against the cabinets in the kitchen, while my middle sister hid under the kitchen table sobbing. I don't remember what happened after that, but Dad must have left because none of us was seriously hurt.

Even though I don't remember some of the details of Dad's abuse, I do remember his being loud, angry, and occasionally violent. Sometimes, he would "tickle" me in the belly as I lay on the living room floor. It would start as a playful gesture, but it would soon turn into a frightening and hurtful one as he wouldn't stop tickling me until I began to cry and begged him to stop.

There were other times when he asked me to scratch his back while he was sitting at the kitchen table, often without a shirt on, and insisted that I do it even when I said I didn't want to. Then, there were the times when I was forced to answer the telephone when bill collectors called, lying and telling the person on the other end of the line that my parents weren't home, even though they were standing next to me, telling me what to say. Lastly, there were the few times that Dad tried to help me with my math homework and belittled me repeatedly when I couldn't understand it.

Mom held the family together and was the disciplinarian. If we did something we weren't supposed to, she would beat us with a wooden paddle—the kind with the rubber ball attached to a rubber band at the end. Mom would remove the ball and the rubber band and "spank" us with the paddle. There were never clear rules to follow, so we never really knew when we were doing something wrong. We just got a beating. When I was 16, I received the last of these beatings. I was so humiliated by my mom's beating me that I finally gathered the courage to tell her she was never to lay a hand on me again.

As I mentioned earlier, I had some good times growing up, playing with my best friend who lived down the street. We would climb trees, play with dolls, play "dress-up," go ice skating on a nearby pond in the winter, adorn ourselves with cherry blossoms in the spring, pretending to be brides, or build forts in the backyard by tossing blankets over a picnic table. Unfortunately, it was during these times of playing in our forts that my best friend sexually abused me. This loss of childhood innocence unconsciously affected me throughout much of my single adult life. I became very promiscuous as a result. However, by God's grace, I was able to forgive myself and my friend later in life, partly because I believe she also experienced sexual abuse at some point.

Somehow, I endured this childhood marked by alcoholism, abuse, humiliation, shame, criticism, and authoritarian control—but with emotional scars that I'm not quite sure have ever fully healed.

BEYOND HIGH SCHOOL

After graduating from high school, I attended college to earn a bachelor's degree in English and nearly completed a master's degree in journalism before my first husband became ill with cancer. I taught 7th and 8th grade English for five years and later edited a professional journal in optometric education. My husband and I had moved to the Washington, D.C. area by then, and shortly after relocating, his Hodgkin's Disease was diagnosed. Following his death, I worked part-time as a secretary for my uncle, who was an architect. Later, I held various temporary and part-time positions as an editor, administrative assistant, and church secretary while raising my children.

I met my second husband while in therapy, trying to cope with my first husband's death. He supported me through the final months of my first husband's illness and passing, and he had become a good friend to my son. As a result, I married him, believing he would be a good father to my son and that we would share a long, happy life together. Unfortunately, things didn't turn out that way. After nearly 20 years of marriage, we divorced. Even though God's intervention in my life had saved me, it seemed to separate me from my second husband. He didn't want to have anything to do with my newfound faith, and I think that eventually drove us apart.

A WILDERNESS MENTALITY

Looking back on this period in my life and the pattern God was showing me, I would say it was a "desert" or "wilderness" phase in my new life. God had saved me, delivered me out of captivity, and demonstrated his miracle-working power to me. However, I was still operating with a "wilderness mentality"—or the wrong mindset.

Joyce Meyer describes a "wilderness mentality" as certain types of wrong thinking that keep a person in bondage.[1] These can be fear, distrust, or unbelief, such as the Israelites struggled with (Deuteronomy 1:7-8, 19-45, Hebrews 3:19). Or they can be

---

1   Joyce Meyer, *Battlefield of the Mind*, Faith Words Edition (New York: Hachette Book Group USA, 2002), 36.

certain attitudes, like basing one's current or future outlook on what one has seen in the past or what one now sees in the present. Joyce calls this "Wilderness Mentality #1: 'My future is determined by my past and my present.'" Joyce says that this mentality kept the Israelites in the wilderness for forty years instead of eleven days because they didn't know how to see with "the eye of faith."

Joyce describes nine additional wilderness mentalities in her book, *The Battlefield of the Mind*. Whatever causes these wrong or negative mindsets, Joyce warns, "a negative outlook leaves a person miserable and unlikely of making any progress toward the Promised Land."[2]

Consequently, as a new Christian being unfamiliar with God, His Word, and His nature, I too was operating with a wilderness mentality—or worldly mindset—that was familiar to me instead of a biblical one based on God's Word. My roots in God were very shallow (Matthew 13:21). I was questioning God's purpose and direction for me, and I was stuck, unable to move forward.

At this point in my journey, I realized I had to choose whether to return to "spiritual Egypt" or face the true state of affairs in my life. I needed to cross the figurative "Jordan River," step into the water, and confront the "giants" in my life (Joshua 3:10-17) in order to move forward to God's Promised Land—the land of His promises for me. I was still quite broken, but I wanted to know God more, and I wanted to be healed.

---

2   Meyer, "Part 3: Wilderness Mentalities," in *Battlefield of the Mind*, 185-196.

The Pattern

THE WILDERNESS MENTALITY

The Israelites wandered in the wilderness for 40 years before reaching the Promised Land because of their unbelief. Even though they saw God's miraculous signs, they struggled to believe they could take the land because they walked by sight rather than faith.

As Christians, we also can fall into a "wilderness mentality" due to wrong mindsets. We may wander aimlessly or even revert to our old ways of life. However, God's Spirit can guide us "into all truth" (John 16:13) and reveal the "giants" we need to face to possess the Promised Land. We just need to stay in faith instead of returning to our old habits.

CHAPTER 5
Crossing the Jordan

> Hear, O Israel: You are now about to cross the Jordan to go in and dispossess nations greater and stronger than you.… The people are strong and tall.… You know about them and have heard it said: "Who can stand up against the [giants]?" But be assured today that the LORD your God is the one who goes across ahead of you like a devouring fire. He will destroy them; he will subdue them before you. And you will drive them out and annihilate them quickly, as the LORD has promised you.

DEUTERONOMY 9:1-3

I remember the day I saw it again—sitting lovingly and treasured in the middle of my newly acquainted pastor's living room. At first glance, it was just an attractive table that caught my eye, but slowly, startlingly, my mind began to realize that this was the same table I had banished to the trash heap about a year earlier.

I was shocked by its restored beauty! The broken, splintered legs had been glued back together; the surface was renewed and polished with barely a trace of refinishing handiwork. In fact, if someone had not seen the table in its former state, they wouldn't even have noticed the slight imperfection in the joint of the crisscrossing bars of the legs, or the missing connecting section that somehow had been replaced and blended to form a complete bond, or the stained and polished top, now smooth and shiny with its inset medallion of lighter wood.

It was whole now, restored by the loving hands of a talented craftsman. I know it was the same table because the pastor proceeded to tell me the story of its origin. A church member had retrieved it from a pile of trash on the street where, unknown to me, she and I both lived. She thought it had the potential to be restored and serve as a useful, beautiful piece of furniture. So, as the words tumbled forth from my pastor's mouth, he recounted the story of how this woman had retrieved it and given it to him.

He knew a craftsman gifted in restoring antiques who he thought might be able to restore it to a semblance of its former beauty.

At that moment, I was utterly astounded by the ironic twist of fate, brought about by a magnificent and loving God! Here was that same table—repaired and restored, resting comfortably and peacefully in the living room of my pastor's house—a symbol of how God had taken hold of my broken life and had begun to redeem it and turn it around.

PANDORA'S BOX

As I read through the Bible in those early years and experienced in my own life what I was reading of the Israelites' journey to the Promised Land, I instinctively adopted a process to transform my thoughts and attitudes that I had learned during my first husband's illness and subsequent death before becoming a Christian.

I had attended a weekend seminar about something called the "New Identity Process," led by an American psychiatrist and psychoanalyst named Dr. Daniel Casriel (d. 1983).[3] We met in a local Montessori preschool that had several classrooms, a kitchen, and a couple of bathrooms. When I entered the meeting room, I saw about 20 to 25 people sitting around in a circle on miniature, child-sized chairs. I guess the setting was somewhat fitting, as I later discovered that the process took me back to childhood memories.

As Dan led the meeting, he began describing his process of releasing suppressed emotions and traumas, which involved bonding and screaming. He had developed this "scream therapy" over a 20-year period during the 1960s and 70s while he served as psychiatric director of AREBA (Accelerated Re-education of Emotions, Behaviors and Attitudes), a private residential therapeutic community in New York City for drug addicts and people with severe character disorders.[4] The genesis of his approach was a visit he made in 1962 to Synanon,[5] a West-Coast community for the rehabilitation of drug addicts and alcoholics, as described in his book, *A Scream Away from Happiness.*[6]

---

3   Wikipedia contributors, "Daniel Harold Casriel," Wikipedia, The Free Encyclopedia, accessed July 4, 2020, https://en.wikipedia.org/wiki/Daniel_Harold_Casriel.

4   The process now is called bonding psychotherapy and is promoted and developed by the International Society for Bonding Psychotherapy (ISBP). "Bonding Psychotherapy: 50 years of history and a look to the future!" Bonding Psychotherapy, accessed July 4, 2020, https://www.bonding-psychotherapy.org/about/what-is-bonding-psychotherapy.

5   Wikipedia contributors, "Synanon," Wikipedia, The Free Encyclopedia, accessed July 4, 2020, https://en.wikipedia.org/wiki/Synanon.

6   Daniel Casriel, M.D., "A Scream Away from Happiness" and "An Analyst's Journey: From Couch to

"When I entered the meeting room, I saw about 20 to 25 people sitting around in a circle on miniature, child-sized chairs. I guess the setting was somewhat fitting, as I later discovered that the process took me back to childhood memories."

Dan's process utilized a form of group psychotherapy that incorporated bonding and screaming to reach deep-seated, often unconscious feelings and attitudes that were fueling a person's dysfunctional behavior. Dan's premise was that human beings had a fundamental need for physical closeness and emotional openness. The bonding process was an accelerated way of feeling safe enough to open up emotionally and to identify more rapidly the feelings, attitudes, and behaviors driving symptoms of disorder.[7]

After Dan introduced the process, we were paired with another member of the group from the circle—often someone of the opposite sex—and sent into another room to "work" the process. During this time, one partner would lie flat on their back while the other partner would lie on top of that person. Each partner took turns lying on top of the other while the one on the bottom would work through their feelings. This was the "bonding" part of the process.

The partner who was lying on top would encourage the one on the bottom to express whatever they were feeling at the time. When it was my turn, I began to express feelings that I was "afraid." My partner then encouraged me to repeat the words, "I'm afraid," louder and louder until I was screaming them. This was the "screaming" part of the process.

Unexpectedly, that day triggered memories from my past. As I screamed louder and louder, I began to experience a fear I had never felt before. It was akin to a primal fear, coming from deep within the recesses of my soul, sometimes gushing out uncontrollably as I screamed louder and louder.

I worked on that feeling and other feelings of pain and anger in a similar fashion throughout the weekend with different group members. As I did, it felt like "Pandora's Box" was opening for me. The process connected me to fear, pain, and anger I had unconsciously buried deep inside me from all the trauma in my life up to that point, leaving me feeling like I would never be the same again.

After a somewhat lengthy period of bonding and screaming, we returned to the meeting room, where Dan began working one-on-one with group members on various feelings that had surfaced during their bonding and screaming. As Dan worked with each individual and identified underlying attitudes that drove their feelings, he encouraged them to replace their negative feelings like "I'm angry" with positive ones like "I'm lovable," "I'm good enough," or "I exist," "I need," and "I'm entitled."

Many people experienced negative feelings caused by abuse, rejection, childhood molestation, or similar issues. Dan encouraged them to express those feelings louder

---

Encounter," in A Scream Away from Happiness (New York: Grosset & Dunlap, 1972) 1-10, 45-65.

7   Casriel, M.D., "The Human Need for Bondedness," in A Scream Away from Happiness, 97-119.

and louder in the group until they were screaming it and then, to replace it with a positive affirmation he suggested, screaming it louder and louder, until it began to take root in their psyche.

I continued attending these weekend workshops and weekly group meetings in the New Identity Process and participated in one-on-one sessions with a licensed psychologist for a number of years to work through the feelings and memories that emerged from my Pandora's Box that day. However, I couldn't work openly in the group meetings for a long time. I was so ashamed of what had happened to me in the past and so overwhelmed with thoughts, feelings, and attitudes I never realized I had, that I couldn't muster the courage to speak up in front of the group. I could only observe and feel empathy for others who had experienced similar things.

A TOOL FOR MY NEWFOUND LIFE

This phase of my life uncovered a lot of repressed feelings about my past. These emotions were shaped by unconscious thoughts and beliefs I had developed over the years, which, in turn, affected my behavior and quality of life. I gradually became aware of these negative feelings, identified the underlying thoughts, attitudes, or beliefs they represented, and recognized how they negatively impacted me.

Although I continued to participate in weekly groups and one-on-one sessions with a licensed psychologist for several years, the benefits of secular therapy were only temporary. Over time, the positive changes in my thoughts, feelings, attitudes, and behavior slowly faded, and I couldn't maintain or regain them, despite my efforts to do so on my own.

I learned one crucial lesson from the New Identity Process, however. It gave me a tool to recognize negative feelings that caused me pain and anger in my new life with Christ. Reflecting on these, I was able to identify the root behind them—the circumstances and the thoughts and beliefs that created those feelings. This was the tool I adopted to help align my thoughts and feelings with God's Word as I read through the Bible in the early years of God's transforming my life.

The process also helped reveal the "giants" I needed to face in order to be healed and restored. God had shown me His unmatched power and ability to help me overcome any enemy I would face, just as He did with the Israelites before they entered the Promised Land. I just had to keep moving forward in faith, trusting that He would help me defeat and destroy them. This gave me the courage to go on.

The Pattern

FACING OUR GIANTS

To reach the Promised Land, the Israelites needed
to cross the Jordan River, face giants in the land, and
dispossess nations greater and stronger than they
were. God had promised to go ahead of them and help
them subdue, drive out, and annihilate their enemies.
All they needed to do was obey the Lord, step into the
water, and cross over to the other side.

In our walk with the Lord, we, too, may need to cross
the figurative Jordan River and face the giants in our
lives to reach God's Promised Land. God's Word assures
us that He will help us overcome them. We must decide
to step into the water, move forward in faith, and trust
Him to help us conquer and destroy them.

CHAPTER 6
Slaying Giants

[The spies] gave Moses this account: "We went into the land to which you sent us, and it does flow with milk and honey! Here is its fruit. But the people who live there are powerful, and the cities are fortified and very large…. The land we explored devours those living in it. All the people we saw there are of great size…. We seemed like grasshoppers in our own eyes, and we looked the same to them."

NUMBERS 13:27-28, 32-33

In ancient Greek mythology, Zeus, the ruler of the gods, gave Pandora a box and warned her not to open it under any circumstances. However, Pandora's curiosity, ironically gifted to her by the gods, compelled her to open the box. Upon doing so, she released all the evil in the world. Only one thing remained inside the box as she hastily closed it, and that was "Hope." Today, the phrase "Pandora's Box" symbolizes doing or starting something that will cause many unforeseen problems, or in a more modern, colloquial meaning, to "open a can of worms."[8]

This also was true of my Pandora's Box that opened during my first workshop in the New Identity Process and in the subsequent years of psychotherapy. At first, it seemed like a small, insignificant action. However, as time passed, I realized that it had far-reaching effects. It unleashed all the evil from my past, while exposing the "giants" I had to conquer in my life.

THE IMPACT OF MY PARENTS

My mother was the catalyst that led me from the New Identity Process to embracing my new identity in Christ. One of the first insights I gained from my Pandora's Box was

---

8   Wikipedia contributors, "Pandora's box," Wikipedia, The Free Encyclopedia, accessed April 18, 2024, https://en.wikipedia.org/wiki/Pandora%27s_box.

my feelings about my mother. I had unconsciously harbored tremendous anger over her lifelong criticisms of me and her attempts to control me—efforts that left me with a poor opinion of myself and low self-esteem. Along with the anger, I harbored a tremendous amount of pain, fear, and guilt. I had developed the belief that perfection was the only way to win Mom's approval and love and to avoid her wrath.

My mother constantly criticized me while growing up—for not standing up straight, not walking fast enough, getting dressed too slowly, not being pushy enough, and so on. She didn't express feelings, and we weren't allowed to either. Her favorite mantra was, "Children should be seen and not heard." Her controlling nature made me more inhibited and fearful of being myself, which led her to criticize me even more.

Even as a married woman with three children, my mother continued to criticize my behavior. Her criticisms made me feel as if nothing I did was ever good enough. When I realized how angry I had been all those years she had suppressed, criticized, and controlled me, it was like lancing an abscess; all the vile feelings of anger, pain, fear, and guilt poured out of me like pus oozing from an infected wound, and this continued for many years.

When I first felt these emotions and reflected on their impact on my life, all I could do was scream and cry. Eventually, as I became more aware of my feelings and what was fueling them, and as I was being discipled in my new life in Christ, I learned that the first step I had to take to be healed was to forgive my mother for all the ways she had hurt me. This I had to do in faith, as I could not bring myself emotionally to forgive the hurt she had caused me.

Forgiving someone in faith, I learned, lifts the burden from the person carrying the hurt and releases it to God to allow Him to work in the situation. Regardless of whether a person deserves forgiveness or not, forgiving someone in faith frees the hurt person from the oppression of their own anger, resentment, and offense, paving the way for healing to begin. Unforgiveness, on the other hand, keeps the hurt person bound by their anger and pain. I will discuss this further in the next chapter.

Along with forgiving my mother, I also needed to repent for judging her as authoritarian and critical and consequently harming me. I realized that, in actuality, I had allowed myself to feel that way because of her behavior (Matthew 7:1-2).

After realizing how my relationship with my mother affected me, my thoughts naturally spilled over to my relationship with my father and the feelings associated with him—primarily those of abandonment, ridicule, and fear. I became afraid of men and the possibility of abuse from them. I also was fearful of ridicule, as my father had impatiently and callously ridiculed me the few times he tried to help me with my math homework. That was the only memory I had of receiving any kind of attention from my father, aside from the abusive "tickling" that I mentioned earlier. I never felt loved by my parents; only unloved and unworthy.

Learning that I Am Loved

The early stages of my new life in Christ felt like a wilderness or desert experience, as noted earlier. For over a year, I endured intense grief and pain, feeling disconnected and cut off from others, as well as incredibly lonely, unloved, and unworthy. I prayed for understanding about what was happening to me and asked God to change my heart or reveal any sin to me. I struggled to accept the truth that God loved me. His Word said He loved me and forgave me, but I felt like such a bad and undeserving person that I didn't see how He could love me.

True to God's faithfulness, He answered my prayers and revealed to me how my behavior was causing feelings of rejection and unworthiness. By judging others as unworthy and believing I was better than them, I was bringing rejection upon myself (Matthew 7:1-2).

God also showed me that feeling unloved is a lie from the enemy. His Word says that I am loved and fearfully and wonderfully made for His purpose (John 3:16; Psalm 139:14). Therefore, I had to repent for believing the lie that I was unloved and ask God to change my heart and heal my wounds.

Some of my early journal entries record these struggles:

July 8: Yesterday, I felt so bad that I prayed for God to show me how to overcome all of the hate I carried toward my parents and my husband for not loving me. God showed me that the answer is forgiveness. His love is perfect toward me, and if I have that, it's all I need. It really doesn't matter whether my parents or my husband love me. Besides, they're not perfect. They had backgrounds that affected their capacity for love or lack of it, and they did the best they knew how. I have to forgive them because they 'knew not what they did.' Understanding how this applies to my husband is harder than understanding how it applies to my parents. I've asked God to allow my heart to accept and forgive even more and to let this grow inside of me.

July 14: I prayed for God's forgiveness for my imperfections and for expecting perfection in others. I prayed to be able to forgive my parents for withholding their love because I was not perfect. I cried quite a bit during church and throughout the afternoon, mourning over this. After church, God sent three people to affirm His love for me. They really poured out God's love toward me. It was very nice, but also very painful. I mourned the loss of my parents' love and my husband's love all afternoon. I realized how perfect God's love is: merciful, faithful, forgiving, and unchanging. It is almost too much to bear because I don't feel worthy of it. But the good news is that I don't have to be perfect. I'm beginning to like myself because of the person I'm becoming. I like the way God is changing me, and I can be loved and worthy without being perfect.

August 4: *I feel at rock bottom, that everything in my life is messed up: my marriage, finances, retirement, friends, and relationships with my kids—even everything I say or do with good intentions. NOTHING IS RIGHT! I've sought my own way, and I can't do it. I can't even be perfect when I try to do the right thing. I need Christ in me to tell me, show me, what to say and do. I also asked God to raise me up, as He did Christ. Thinking about what Jesus had to endure gives me hope, faith, and strength. I can endure anything of the world if I have Christ alive in me. I think that is what produces an abundant life in God's terms: peace, joy, and love.*

There are two childish attitudes stopping me from loving others and keeping me wounded. One is unrealistic expectations (and hidden expectations) that my parents, loved ones, friends, neighbors, or even God should or ought to behave in certain ways. This creates disappointment and a wounded heart. The answer is repentance of this childish attitude and forgiveness of others and myself, as well as asking God to forgive me and to change my heart. That is our commandment —forgiveness. All fall short of the glory of God and yet are loved and forgiven.

The second childish attitude is rebellion—an 'I'll show them' attitude if they don't love me or want me. 'I'll get something they want and make them jealous.' I must repent of trying to get even. Only the Lord can claim justice; only the Lord can rightly judge. We must forgive all trespasses, again realizing that all fall short, that we are forgiven, and that Jesus is our only Lord and Savior. Only God is

perfect…. It takes a tremendous amount of self-control, compassion, love, and adult thinking to suspend childish beliefs and act more like Christ. I think this can only be done with God's help—complete trust, faith, and hope in God.

September 8: *I am coming out of a negative, self-centered love—believing that I have suffered for many years and will continue to suffer, that I am unworthy and unloved, and that I am rejected by all. I have been feeling sorry for myself. God is showing me that He loved me first, that He is conforming me into the image of Christ, and that my sufferings are discipline leading me to maturity and raising me to be the kind of person He wants me to be: someone who can love and serve others. He is changing my view from a negative, self-centered one to a positive, 'other-centered' one. A friend told me that I am a friendly person, that the spirit* *of rejection is from the devil, and that if others reject me, it is because they have a problem. Praise God!*

September 26: *I am coming out of a season (period) of feeling rejection, pain, and self-pity. I have proclaimed victory over the pain, some of which I caused myself and some I suffered at the hands of those I loved (my parents and my husband). God has shown me that all my suffering was necessary to mold me into the kind of person He wanted me to be—to serve Him and understand that He has given me a rich blessing (He answers all of my prayers). What would have been easily gained would have been easily lost. Now, I can sit at the banqueting table and enjoy the meal. 'Because he himself suffered when He was tempted, he is able to help those who are being tempted' (Hebrews 2:18). This is what happened to me. Now, I am ready to help those being tempted, and I am ready for God to help me with fear.*

APPLYING THE TOOLS

As I learned to identify my feelings and the thoughts driving them, I also learned to use the tools gained from the New Identity Process to change my thinking. First, I learned to recognize my feelings in any situation. Second, I learned to search for and identify their root causes—the attitudes and beliefs connected to the feelings. Third, I learned to measure those attitudes and beliefs against the Word of God, which is the ultimate truth. Finally, I learned to forgive, repent, or come out of agreement with any lies I was believing and to ask God to forgive, cleanse, and heal me.

In my early walk as a believer, I was able to replace negative thoughts and feelings with positive ones I gleaned from the Word of God through my own efforts. After a few years of doing this, however, I grew extremely weary of working to change myself. At the same time, I also was frustrated because I couldn't make any further progress. One day, a highly perceptive pastor visited our church, and I had a chance to talk with him about it. He suggested that I let go and allow God to change me. So, I decided to trust my loving heavenly Father to bring about any further change.

At some point during my Bible reading journey, I reached the Book of Joshua and decided to figuratively put my foot into the Jordan River and cross into the Promised Land—or the land of God's promises in my life. I understood that if I didn't cross the Jordan and confront the hurts and demons from my past, I never would be healed or enter God's land flowing with milk and honey that He promised in His Word. With my pastor's permission, I began to meet with an older woman in the church who had offered to disciple me regularly. Thus, I embarked on what became a seven-year effort to slay the giants from my past.

The Pattern

CONQUERING OUR GIANTS

The Israelites learned that the Promised Land was truly a land flowing with milk and honey. However, they also discovered they would face large, fortified cities and people of great size and strength (giants), which led them to view themselves as grasshoppers.

The giants we must face may seem formidable or impossible, but the only way to become all that God wants us to be is to cross the figurative Jordan River and slay the giants that prevent us from entering the Promised Land. If we don't address these demons from our past, we may never reach God's land of milk and honey that He promises in His Word.

CHAPTER 7
Forgiveness

In spite of all this, [the Israelites] kept on sinning; in spite of his wonders, they did not believe.... Yet he was merciful; he forgave their iniquities and did not destroy them. Time after time he restrained his anger and did not stir up his full wrath. He remembered that they were but flesh, a passing breeze that does not return.

PSALM 78:32, 38-39

Seven years after I began slaying the giants from my past, my life changed dramatically. My husband and I divorced, which meant I needed to re-enter the workforce after a 12-year absence. My two younger children faced several problems in high school. So, I opted to homeschool my youngest son while working, and my middle son went to live with his father.

By the grace of God, I found a position as an editor for an organization that developed and taught Bible study curriculum. After working there for two years, they moved out of state, and I had to find another job. I then secured a position with an information technology company, working as a writer and editor on government proposals. Since I was working and homeschooling my youngest child in my spare time, I didn't have much time to nurture my relationship with God.

As things began to settle and I adjusted to my new life, I realized I still felt a large hole of emptiness in my heart that hadn't healed. One day, a friend suggested I join her at a nearby church for a program called Celebrate Recovery.[9] Celebrate Recovery is a Christ-centered recovery program based on eight principles from "The Beatitudes" found in Jesus' "Sermon on the Mount" (Matthew 5:1-12). It was founded in 1991 as a ministry of Saddleback Church in Lake Forest, CA by Pastors John and Cheryl Baker.[10]

---

9 Celebrate Recovery is a Christ-centered recovery program based on eight principles from the "Beatitudes" found in Jesus' "Sermon on the Mount" (Matthew 5:1-12). The principles correspond to the 12 Steps of AA (Alcoholics Anonymous) and are further described in the *Celebrate Recovery Leader's Guide* (John Baker, *Celebrate Recovery Leader's Guide*, [Grand Rapids, Michigan: Zondervan, 1998, 2005] 9-19).

10 "About Us: Our History," Celebrate Recovery, accessed August 13, 2024, https://celebraterecovery.com/about.

LEARNING ABOUT FORGIVENESS

When my friend and I attended my first meeting, everyone introduced themselves by saying, "Hello. I am [name], a grateful believer in Jesus Christ." My heart sank. I couldn't repeat the words, "I am a grateful believer in Jesus Christ." At that moment, I didn't feel at all like a grateful believer. I had lost my marriage, been forced to reenter the workforce, and was barely making enough money to pay my bills—my family was broken and so was my heart. I was a believer, but I couldn't say that I was a *grateful* believer. This showed me I still had more work to do within myself.

As mentioned earlier, one of the first steps I learned that I needed to take to find healing was to forgive those who had hurt me. Celebrate Recovery also taught this lesson. Without forgiveness, a person can't move forward from people, things, or events that have hurt them or things they may have done to themselves or others. I had worked on forgiving my parents when I was discipled by the older woman from my church. However, as I worked through the lessons and the program in Celebrate Recovery, I learned even more about forgiveness.

Forgiveness is the foundation of our relationship with God. The Bible says that *"While we were still sinners, Christ died for us"* (Romans 5:8). In Celebrate Recovery's lesson on forgiveness, the program's founder, Pastor John Baker, explains that God's forgiveness is "the first and most important forgiveness…extended from God to us…. By His [Jesus'] death on the cross, all our sins were canceled, paid in full; a free gift for those who believe in Him as the true and only Higher Power, Savior, and Lord."[11] Pastor Baker also emphasizes that to be completely free from our resentments, anger, fears, shame, or guilt, we need to "give and accept forgiveness in all areas of [our] lives."[12]

Forgiveness is a fundamental command that Jesus gave to believers. In the book of Matthew, Jesus says, *"For if you forgive men when they sin against you, your heavenly Father will also forgive you. But if you do not forgive men their sins, your Father will not forgive your sins"* (Matthew 6:14-15). Forgiveness also transfers the responsibility of retribution into the capable hands of God, who promises that He will repay (Romans 12:19).

Since forgiveness is a command, I learned that we must forgive others even if we can only do so initially through faith and obedience to God's Word. Often, it's difficult to forgive someone who truly has hurt us, especially when we think they should have known better or when they show no remorse. However, we cannot be the judge and jury of the situation. The person who hurt us may not be aware of what they did or

---

11   Baker, *Celebrate Recovery Leader's Guide*, 165.
12   Baker, *Celebrate Recovery Leader's Guide*, 165.

may not even care. The verdict remains the same: unforgiveness hurts us, not them. Carrying seeds of anger, resentment, fear, shame, or guilt harms us, and those seeds continue to grow until they devour our peace and progress. Replaying the hurt in our heads only draws us further into the depths of unforgiveness and despair.

I also learned that if we must first forgive someone in faith rather than from the heart, we can ask God to help us reach a point where we truly can forgive them from the heart. Forgiving in faith allows God to work in our situation, releasing us to a place where we can let go of the past and receive healing and deliverance.

Over time, God imparts new revelation that begins to transform our hearts, gives us new perspectives, and enables us to truly forgive from the heart. Forgiveness may require multiple attempts before we are completely free from the defilement of the hurt. Jesus said we are to forgive *"...not seven times, but seventy-seven times"* (Mathew 18:22). It is kind of like peeling an onion one layer at a time. In the end, we are more able to come to a place of forgiveness and acceptance, knowing that God works all things *"for the good of those who love Him, who have been called according to His purpose"* (Romans 8:28).

Forgiveness and unforgiveness also have a compounding quality that creates ripple effects within relationships. When we forgive and follow God's command to love one another, it yields the fruits of the Spirit within us—love, joy, peace, patience, kindness, goodness, faithfulness, gentleness, and self-control (Galatians 5:22-23). On the other hand, if we perpetuate unforgiveness, remain hurt, and consequently hurt others, it produces anger, hatred, discord, jealousy, dissension, and more, which are fruits of our sinful nature (Galatians 5:19-21). This inhibits love from flowing through us to others, and the hurt is passed on from us to others.

It is important to understand that forgiving is not the same as excusing the harm done to us. Pastor Baker reminds us: "You will not find the peace and freedom from your persecutors until you are able to forgive them. Remember, forgiving them in no way excuses them for the harm they caused you, but it will release you from the power they have had over you."[13] We forgive because it is a command, and doing so releases the power the other person has over us.

It also is important to remember that the harm others cause us is born of their free will—it is not God's will. That person's past experiences might have influenced their actions that hurt us. On the other hand, their own fleshly desires might have influenced them, but the outcome is Satan's will, not God's.

---

13   Baker, *Celebrate Recovery Leader's Guide*, 166-167.

A More Compassionate Perspective

Over time, God worked to change my heart as I forgave my parents, first in faith, and then multiple times over, for the hurt I thought I experienced as a child. I felt so harmed by my mother's harsh criticism and discipline, as well as the threatening and abusive behavior of my father, that I thought I never could forgive either of them for what they had done to me. Once I understood that forgiveness preceded healing, I did so and asked God to help me truly forgive them and to change my heart.

Eventually, God *did* change my heart, and I was able to forgive them fully. I realized that aspects of my parents' lives, circumstances, and upbringing likely influenced the way they treated me, and this also affected the environment in which I was raised. Slowly, I gained a more compassionate perspective toward them and was able to forgive them from my heart.

It dawned on me that being married to an alcoholic meant my mother spent most of my childhood as a single parent of four children. She spent a lot of time rescuing my father and struggling with our home life. Since I was the oldest, she needed my help with my siblings while she worked every day to support us. She often commented that she thought this was her cross to bear. I never understood why she believed that, but for some reason, she did, and that's what she lived by.

My father was an intelligent, compassionate, and kind human being. However, he struggled with an alcohol addiction, which brought pain, misery, shame, and abandonment into our lives. For this reason, I could never quite forgive him while he was still alive. He eventually renounced alcoholism and gave his heart to Jesus Christ, but I still could not bring myself to forgive his actions or behavior in the past. My sister once heard him comment, "Christ has forgiven me for my sins; why can't my daughters forgive me?"

It took many years before I could begin to imagine the suffering my father had endured throughout his life and to forgive him from my heart. I don't know why I couldn't forgive him sooner. Something always kept me from surrendering that forgiveness up to the very moment of his death and beyond. Perhaps it was unrealistic expectations—wanting him to admit he was sorry for all he had done—or maybe it was something else. Whatever the reason, I realized that I was foolish in that respect. My unforgiveness had made me just as foolish, blind, and selfish as I accused him of being. It kept the two of us from reconciliation, and it kept me apart from someone I loved. My unforgiveness had hurt him also.

Asking Others for Forgiveness

In addition to forgiving those who have hurt us, I learned that we also may have

"Eventually, God did change my heart, and I was able to forgive them fully. I realized that aspects of my parents' lives, circumstances, and upbringing likely influenced the way they treated me, and this also affected the environment in which I was raised. "

caused harm to others or ourselves. Celebrate Recovery taught me that we need to ask for forgiveness from those we have hurt and do what we can to make amends, if making amends won't hurt the other person or ourselves.[14]

The Bible says that *"all have sinned and fall short of the glory of God"* (Romans 3:23). We might not understand why we hurt others or ourselves, but it really doesn't matter. The simple fact is we did it, and we probably didn't know any better. I believe that may be what Jesus meant when he was nailed to the cross and said, *"Father, forgive them, for they do not know what they are doing"* (Luke 23:34). Even if we could fathom all things to the end of time, would we know any better? I doubt it because we, unlike God, are not perfect.

I also learned that we need to examine whether we are angry, resentful, or blaming God for our pain. This is another area where forgiveness may be necessary. We may have blamed God for something that happened to us or for something we caused ourselves. For a long time, I blamed God for the death and loss of my first husband until I realized that I needed to repent for blaming God and ask Him to forgive me. Only then could I begin to heal from that hurt.

God is perfect; He doesn't make mistakes. James 1:17 tells us that *"Every good and perfect gift is from above, coming down from the Father of the heavenly lights, who does not change like shifting shadows."* Blaming God would be finding fault with Him or holding Him responsible for something that is not His will. Pastor Baker reminds us that God "loved us so much that He gave us a free will. He didn't want us to be His puppets. He wanted us to love Him as our choice. [We] need to understand and believe that the harm others did to [us] was from their free will. It was their choice, not God's. It was *not* God's will."[15]

Forgiveness is not an easy thing to do. It requires us to set aside our own self-interests, humble ourselves before God, and remember that our sins have been forgiven through the death of His Son, Jesus Christ, who first loved us while we were still sinners (Romans 5:8). It calls us to see the situation from Christ's point of view: to love the other person despite what they have done and to forgive them because it is Christ's command and because they truly may not know what they have done (Matthew 6:14-15, Luke 23:34).

Although we are not perfect, we are called to a high standard of perfection (Matthew 5:48) and to imitate God's love and forgiveness (Ephesians 4:32-5:2). The apostle Paul wrote, *"Love does no harm to its neighbor"* (Romans 13:10) and love *"keeps no record of*

---

14   Baker, *Celebrate Recovery Leader's Guide,* 167.
15   Baker, *Celebrate Recovery Leader's Guide,* 166.

wrongs" (1 Corinthians 13:5). In other words, love includes forgiveness, even to the point of loving and forgiving one's enemies (Matthew 5:44, 6:14-15, Mark 11:25).

DEALING WITH RESIDUAL PAIN

Sometimes, despite all we do to forgive, let go, and move on with our lives, we still may carry residual pain that only God can heal. This was true for me. I had been hurt by many things in my life—particularly, my father's abuse and abandonment, my mother's extensive criticism, the loss of my first husband, and the abandonment of my second husband. Even though I forgave them and myself for anything that might have caused the hurt from these experiences, the pain still remained within me.

One day, a friend described how God had given her a vision of the blood of Jesus cleansing her by flowing through her body like through the trunk of a tree and spreading into all the major and secondary roots connected to her. When I spent time alone with God that day, I decided to pray and ask Him to remove the pain that remained in me from these experiences, no matter what it took. I had endured enough!

Shortly after I presented this request to Him, while still praying, I saw a similar vision of the blood of Jesus flowing through me like through the trunk of a tree and spreading into all of my major and secondary roots. Then, the blood began to pour over me, leaving me completely drenched and saturated. I felt as though it was coming from Heaven, much like when the Holy Spirit descended upon Jesus after His baptism (Matthew 3:16). The blood turned into a thick gel and then into a metal-hard suit of armor that completely covered me. When it was finished, I had the sense that a suit of armor made from the blood of Jesus had completely covered me and cleansed me from all residual pain. My armor stood ready to protect me from all harm from that point on. God had accomplished something that only He could do in my life.

The Red Sea crossing, water from the rock, manna and quail—all were miracles that God used to demonstrate His divine protection, provision, love, and compassion for the Israelites. Still, they doubted, complained, and wanted to return to Egypt, even going as far as making an idol of a golden calf (Numbers 21:5, Exodus 32:4). In His mercy, God continued to lead them to the land He had promised they would receive, even though His anger burned against them for their disobedience. His magnificent love, forgiveness, and compassion for their human frailties were clearly evident in His response toward them. This is how we should live with one another.

The Pattern

EXTENDING FORGIVENESS

God performed many miracles to demonstrate His divine love, protection, and provision for the Israelites. Yet, they continued to sin against Him and persisted in unbelief. God, in His infinite mercy, restrained His anger, forgave their iniquities, and did not destroy them. He continued to lead them to the land He had promised in spite of His anger toward them.

On our journey to God's Promised Land, one of the first things many of us may need to do is forgive those who have hurt us. Forgiveness is a basic key to healing and deliverance in our lives. Without forgiveness, we can't move past the people or situations that have hurt us. God extended forgiveness to us while we were still sinners. We need to do the same.

CHAPTER 8
Rebuilding the Temple

See, I set before you today life and prosperity, death and destruction. For I command you today to love the LORD your God, to walk in his ways, and to keep his commands, decrees and laws; then you will live and increase, and the LORD your God will bless you in the land you are entering to possess…. Now choose life, so that you and your children may live….

DEUTERONOMY 30:15-16, 19

God intended to establish the Israelites as His holy people to demonstrate to all peoples on Earth that those who are called by the name of the Lord would enjoy blessings, life, and abundant prosperity if they would love the Lord, walk in obedience to Him, and carefully follow all His commands (Deuteronomy 28:10, 1-14). That was His covenant blessing with them. He chose them as a treasured possession to testify to the world of His extraordinary faithfulness and covenant-keeping love (Deuteronomy 7:6, 9; 14:2).

However, if the Israelites disobeyed God's commands, Moses warned them that curses would come upon them, including wasting diseases, sudden ruin, cruel oppression, devouring locusts, and the loss of sons and daughters (Deuteronomy 28:15-57). God's people would *"find no repose, no resting place for the sole of* [their] *foot,"* and they would develop *"an anxious mind, eyes weary with longing, and a despairing heart"* (Deuteronomy 28:64-68). Thus, the Israelites were given a choice between blessing and cursing, life and death.

Like the Israelites, I believe that we, too, have a choice between blessing and cursing, life and death. The Bible tells us in Romans that:

Letting your sinful nature control your mind leads to death. But letting the Spirit control your mind leads to life and peace. For the sinful nature is always hostile to God. It never did obey God's laws, and it never will. That's why those who are still under the control of their sinful nature can never please God. But you are not controlled by your sinful nature. You are controlled by the Spirit if you have the Spirit of God living in you. (And remember that those who do not have the Spirit of Christ living in them do not belong to him at all.)

ROMANS 8:6-9 (NLT)

As believers, we are new creations in Christ (2 Corinthians 5:17) and have been predestined to be conformed to the likeness of God's Son (Romans 8:29). The Bible also says that our bodies are temples of the Holy Spirit (1 Corinthians 6:19). Considering that, it is essential that we rebuild our temples—our bodies. That involves renewing our minds with God's Word and cultivating new mindsets that reflect the spiritual mind of Christ we now possess, rather than our fleshly minds that were shaped by the world.

Romans 12:2 instructs us, *"Do not conform any longer to the pattern of this world, but be transformed by the renewing of your mind. Then you will be able to test and approve what God's will is—his good, pleasing and perfect will."* If we want to understand God's will and experience His blessings for our lives, we need to renew our minds so we can think and act in a way that aligns with His Word and His perspective. Philippians 4:8 also urges us: *"Finally, brothers, whatever is true, whatever is noble, whatever is right, whatever is pure, whatever is lovely, whatever is admirable—if anything is excellent or praiseworthy—think about such things."*

Jesus further illustrates this point with the example of new wineskins: *"And no one pours new wine into old wineskins. If he does, the wine will burst the skins, and both the wine and the wineskins will be ruined. No, he pours new wine into new wineskins"* (Mark 2:22). Jesus is explaining that we need to develop new wineskins—or new mindsets—that reflect God's Word and nature and let go of our old wineskins, or mindsets that were shaped by the world. In this way, God can pour His new wine—His will, thoughts, guidance, revelation, etc.—into us. In fact, one of the ways Jesus shed His blood for us prior to His crucifixion was by allowing a crown of thorns to be driven into his head (Matthew 27:29), a representation of the redemption of our carnal minds. That makes the renewing of our minds pretty important!

A wise pastor I know once said, "The obstacles in our lives are like walls. We can go around them, over them, or tunnel under them. But to avoid the situation means it's still there. To be all that God has ordained us to be, it's best to break right through the wall. Therefore, that issue never stands in the way again—be it fear, anxiety, anger, age, race, etc."[16] Renewing our minds enables us to overcome our circumstances instead of remaining victims of lies or negative experiences.

---

16   Rev. Douglas Dyer, Jr., *Facebook*, January 11, 2021, https://www.facebook.com.

ACQUIRING NEW MINDSETS

To renew our minds and adopt new mindsets, we must decide, like the Israelites had to do, to believe and obey God's Word (which results in "blessing" and "life"), rather than remain in our old thought patterns (which leads to "cursing" and "death"). This crucial step determines the way we speak, behave, and live, which in turn determines the course of our lives. Proverbs 23:7 says, *"For as* [a man] *thinks in his heart, so **is** he"* (NKJV), and Proverbs 4:23 instructs us, *"Above all else, guard your heart, for everything you do flows from it"* (NIV).

Renewing your mind requires faith, according to Kenneth Copeland Ministries. An article on the website explains that "faith is acting on the Word of God… just as you would act on the word of any honest man. You apply it in order to change the way you think about your life, your work, your relationships—everything." God's Word provides a way "for you to be changed from the inside out" and "allows you to know Him and approach your life in a way that pleases Him." Renewing your mind with God's Word "brings your will into agreement with the Father's will" and you begin to think and act in a way that pleases Him. "When difficulties or decisions arise, you automatically view them through the eyes of God's Word. That new perspective changes everything."[17]

Reflecting on my journey, I realized that almost every change God wanted to make in me began with a choice I had to make—a decision made in faith. For example, at the beginning of my walk with God, I had to ***choose to believe in faith*** that I was saved through Jesus' death on the cross. When I read and studied God's Word, I had to ***choose to believe in faith*** that what the Bible said was true. When I asked God to remove my double-mindedness, I had to ***choose to believe in faith*** that He would answer my prayer and trust Him for the outcome, no matter what happened. When I asked God to help me believe that He loved me, He showed me that I had to ***choose to believe in faith*** that He does love me.

As I worked to renew my mind as a new believer, I developed a process to identify my feelings and get to the root of them in order to change my thinking. I also learned to use the tools I previously had gained in the New Identity Process to help me identify thoughts, attitudes, and beliefs that conflicted with the Word of God and to use those tools to renew my thinking with God's truth. The following is a description of that process.

---

17   "What Does It Mean to 'Renew My Mind'?" Kenneth Copeland Ministries, accessed September 19, 2025, https://www.kcm.org/real-help/spiritual-growth/apply/what-does-it-mean-renew-my-mind?language_content_entity=en-US.

A Believer's Process for Renewing the Mind

In working this process, it is crucial that it begins with a strong belief in the saving grace of God's Son, Jesus Christ. It also requires a solid understanding of the Word of God and an unwavering commitment to renewing the mind and obeying God's Word. Additionally, it involves dedicating time to meditate on personal experiences and allow the Holy Spirit to reveal feelings, thoughts, attitudes, and beliefs necessary to guide you through the process and facilitate a transformation in thinking.

The process also demands a great deal of faith and perseverance, because the situations the Lord uses to transform us are not always pleasant; in fact, they can be rather painful and exhausting. Still, they lead to a wonderful harvest of joy and peace.

Step 1: Identify Your Feelings

Whenever something happens that upsets or bothers you, first determine exactly what you're feeling about the incident or situation. Are you angry, hurt, sad, disappointed, fearful, rejected, or offended? For example, if I came home from work upset after an encounter with a co-worker, I would reflect on the situation and ask myself, "What exactly am I feeling about the situation?" If I determined the emotion was anger, I would then move on to Step 2.

Step 2: Identify the Cause of Your Feelings

Once you recognize the emotion, ask, "Why do I feel this way? What attitude, thought, or belief is behind it?" In the example above, I would ask myself, "Why am I angry about what happened with that co-worker? Do I feel rejected or ignored? What is causing my anger?" After reflecting on the situation, I might realize that my anger stemmed from the belief that my coworker didn't listen to me, or that I felt rejected.

Step 3: Identify the Source of the Thought, Attitude, or Belief

After you determine what is driving the feeling, ask yourself, "Where does that thought, attitude, or belief come from? Is it something from childhood or a past experience?" This usually reveals the root of the feeling—its source—and the thought, attitude, or belief behind it.

Using the example above, after some reflection, I might recognize that I felt angry because the situation reminded me of times in my childhood when I felt ignored or rejected by my parents. This led me to project similar attitudes and feelings onto the interaction with my coworker, even though this may have been inaccurate. My reaction stemmed from a learned belief rooted in past experiences, and my mind automatically and unconsciously responded in a similar way.

Once the root is revealed, it becomes easier to address the issue and renew your thinking because you know the source of the problem. It is crucial that the root cause be addressed in order to renew your mind, see the situation clearly, and avoid getting angry again (or having the same response) when a similar situation arises in the future.

Step 4: Identify Biblical Truth

Next, ask, "What does God's Word say about this?" God's Word contains the truth for any situation you face. The truth is not a feeling, belief, or attitude you hold. **The truth is what God's Word says about you and your situation.** Applying this step requires a working knowledge of God's Word to assess biblical truth.

Continuing with our example above, God's Word says to *"Get rid of all bitterness, rage and anger, brawling and slander, along with every form of malice"* (Ephesians 4:31), and to forgive those who hurt you (Colossians 3:13). Consequently, I would need to recognize that my anger and unforgiveness toward my parents and my co-worker did not align with the Word of God, and I would need to replace my thinking with a biblical truth about anger and unforgiveness to renew my mind in that area.

Step 5: Correct the Attitude or Belief

Once the truth is identified, ask, "How can I renew my mind in this area using biblical truth?" You may need to: (1) repent of a sin; (2) forgive someone or yourself; (3) repent for believing a lie and come out of agreement with it; or (4) pray and ask God to cleanse and change your heart.

In our example, God's Word says to eliminate all **anger** and to forgive one another *"just as in Christ God forgave you"* (Ephesians 4:31-32). As a result, I would need to repent for being angry with my parents and my co-worker and ask God to forgive me and cleanse me. In addition, I would need to forgive my parents and my co-worker for what I perceived as their neglect or rejection.

Step 6: Pray

Spend time in prayer. Repent for harboring anger toward those involved. Ask the Lord to help you forgive others and pray that He will forgive and cleanse you from all unrighteousness (1 John 1:9).

As you reach this stage in the process, and perhaps see the situation more clearly, you may even recognize that those involved were not at fault. In our example, maybe my co-worker *was* listening to me. This would require me to repent for believing the lie that he/she wasn't listening and to come out of agreement with it (2 Corinthians 10:5; James 4:7). Alternatively, I might conclude that my co-worker *wasn't* listening to me. In that case, forgiveness would be warranted. I would need to pray and ask God to help me forgive and ask that He would bless them (Luke 6:27-28).

After spending some time praying for forgiveness and cleansing, ask God to lead you into all truth as He renews your mind with His Word. This is where the *real* work begins!

Step 7: Be Watchful and Intentional When Addressing This Pattern As It Arises

It now becomes your responsibility to work with the Holy Spirit daily to renew your mind in the area(s) you've identified. This requires a vigilant attitude. As Joyce Meyer says, "Think about what you're thinking about."[18] Every time the old feeling, thought, or belief comes to mind, take it captive, forgive again if necessary, or reject the lie, and **confess the truth of God's Word instead** (2 Corinthians 10:5).

It's vital to continue to **confess (speak aloud) God's Word** and believe it in faith. Remember, your thoughts determine the course of your life (Proverbs 23:7, 4:23; Matthew 15:19 NLT), and the power of life and death is in your tongue (Proverbs 18:21). What's more, the way to triumph over your accuser, the devil, is through the word of your testimony (Revelation 12:11). Don't let your guard down, because the devil's goal is to steal, kill, and destroy you by capitalizing on every negative thought that comes along (John 10:10).

When negative thoughts persist and become overwhelming, exercise your spiritual authority and cast down imaginations by speaking words of truth found in 2 Corinthians 10:5: "*We demolish arguments and every pretension that sets itself up against the knowledge of God, and we take captive every thought to make it obedient to Christ.*" For me, confessing this scripture aloud sent the devil running every time!

Step 8: Regularly Evaluate Your Position

Once you have developed a habit of taking every thought captive and renewing it with God's Word, continue to be watchful and hold onto your faith and confession. In the book of Revelation, Jesus warned the churches in Thyatira and Philadelphia to hold onto what they had received (Revelation 2:25, 3:11). You need to put on your armor every day, be alert, and continue to stand against the schemes of the devil (Ephesians

---

18   Meyer, "Think About What You're Thinking About," in *Battlefield of the Mind*, 63-69.

6:10-18). Satan uses many tactics to plant seeds of doubt. We'll discuss more of his tactics in the next chapter.

As part of my journey, I continued working on issues identified in the Celebrate Recovery program for about six or seven more years. Using the process outlined above, I was able to overcome wrong thinking and acting caused by depression, fear, codependency, love addiction, being an adult child of an alcoholic, and childhood abuse acquired from my past. I also served on the Celebrate Recovery leadership team, taught various lessons in the large group meetings, and shared my testimony. In addition, I led small groups for open sharing and step study work, helping others overcome hurts, hangups, and destructive habits they faced. It's amazing what God can do to change a person just by sitting around a table or a small group circle and sharing and listening to what others and we ourselves are struggling with.

Admittedly, this process of renewing the mind requires a significant amount of time, self-reflection, and practice. It is like tearing down and rebuilding the temple of God within us, brick by brick. It has taken me many years to overcome much of the worldly thinking acquired from my past, and I am still in the process of renewing my mind in certain areas. However, the Bible says that God wants us to grow in the Lord:

> Until we all reach unity in the faith and in the knowledge of the Son of God and become mature, attaining to the whole measure of the fullness of Christ. Then we will no longer be infants, tossed back and forth by the waves, and blown here and there by every wind of teaching and by the cunning and craftiness of men in their deceitful scheming. Instead, speaking the truth in love, we will in all things grow up into him, who is the Head, that is, Christ.

EPHESIANS 4:13-15

Because of this, I prefer to keep working toward changing my thinking to positive views that produce blessings and life rather than holding on to negative views instilled by the world that would keep me in bondage to anger, fear, hurt, offense, etc., and eventually bring cursing and death (Romans 6:23).

The Pattern

REBUILDING OUR TEMPLES

To receive God's covenant blessings, life, and abundant prosperity, the Israelites had to love the Lord, walk in obedience, and carefully follow all His commands. However, if they did not obey His commands, curses would befall them. In this way, they were given a choice between blessing and cursing, life and death.

We also face a choice between blessing and cursing, life and death. If we want to experience the Lord's blessing and abundant life that He has promised, we need to renew our minds to become more like Christ and surrender our old, worldly patterns of thinking. Renewing our minds is vital to rebuilding our temples because our thoughts shape the way we speak, act, and live, which in turn affects the course of our lives.

CHAPTER 9
Facing Opposition

When the LORD your God brings you into the land you are entering
to possess and drives out before you many nations…seven nations larger
and stronger than you—and when the LORD your God has delivered
them over to you and you have defeated them, then you must destroy
them totally.

DEUTERONOMY 7:1-2

On this journey of renewing my mind and becoming all that God called me to be, I've learned that challenges are inevitable. The Bible tells us that we will have troubles, but Jesus has overcome them all: *"I have told you these things, so that in me you may have peace,"* Jesus says. *"In this world you will have trouble. But take heart! I have overcome the world"* (John 16:33). Different versions of the Bible translate the word "trouble" as "tribulation," "distress," "trials," "suffering," and "persecution."

No matter what challenges we face, they serve a good purpose. They change and form us into who Christ wants us to be (James 1:2-3). Also, like the Israelites in the desert, the pressures keep us moving toward the destination God has for us. In 2 Corinthians 3:18 (NASB), the Bible tells us that we are being gradually transformed into the likeness of Christ with ever-increasing glory: *"But we all, with unveiled faces, looking as in a mirror at the glory of the Lord, are being transformed into the same image from glory to glory, just as from the Lord, the Spirit."*

LITTLE BY LITTLE

God knows what He is doing in our lives, and we need to trust Him. The Bible explains that God allowed enemies to remain in the Promised Land so the Israelites wouldn't forget how to fight and to test their obedience to the Lord's commands:

These are the nations the LORD left to test all those Israelites who had not experienced any of the wars in Canaan (he did this only to teach warfare to the descendants of the Israelites who had not had previous battle experience).... They were left to test the Israelites to see whether they would obey the LORD's commands, which he had given their forefathers through Moses.

JUDGES 3:1-4

The Bible also says that God would only give the Israelites a little land at a time; otherwise, the wild animals would overtake them:

I will send my terror ahead of you and throw into confusion every nation you encounter. I will make all your enemies turn their backs and run...But I will not drive them out in a single year, because the land would become desolate and the wild animals too numerous for you. Little by little I will drive them out before you, until you have increased enough to take possession of the land.

EXODUS 23:27, 29-30

I believe the "wild animals" symbolize challenges we will face or changes we will need to make in order to grow, strengthen our faith, and possess the Promised Land in our lives. If we tried to overcome all of our giants at once, it would be too much for us. Consequently, we will need to fight the good fight of faith (1 Timothy 6:12) to meet and overcome these challenges, but they will not overcome us. As we continue to walk by faith, we will learn to overcome them, little by little, as we grow in the Lord.

In writing this book, I had to overcome many challenges. I learned that trusting God and obeying His Word are very important in accomplishing anything He's called us to do. When I first gave my life back to the Lord and began reading the Bible, God showed me a vision of writing this book. I didn't begin writing the first draft until almost 15 years later. Another 15 years passed, and I was still working to complete it.

Similar to how the Israelites took forty years to cross the desert into the Promised Land—a journey that should have taken less than two weeks—a myriad of things delayed my writing. Every time I started to work on this book, something would happen to prevent me from writing—health issues, learning challenges, getting my children successfully through school, navigating a divorce, returning to full-time employment, working through my own recovery, selling my house, and retiring to another state.

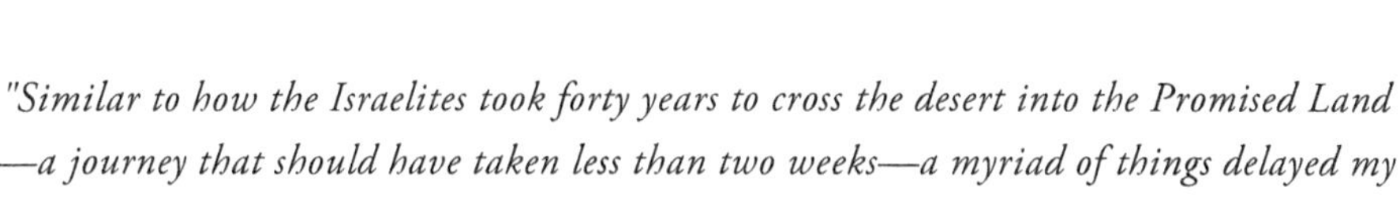

"Similar to how the Israelites took forty years to cross the desert into the Promised Land —a journey that should have taken less than two weeks—a myriad of things delayed my writing. Every time I started to work on this book, something would happen to prevent me from writing..."

I made small steps toward completing this book over the years, adding more content with each revision. After ten years had passed, however, the hope of completing the dream started to fade. Then I saw something posted from another ministry that encouraged me: *"As the body without the spirit is dead, so faith without deeds is dead"* (James 2:26).[19] That was the answer I needed! I had to step out in faith and begin writing again, trusting God with the outcome despite facing serious health challenges.

Sometimes what seems like a detour actually can be God's protection. The Bible says that God led the Israelites on the longer route through the desert toward the Red Sea to protect them: *"For God said, 'If they face war, they may change their minds and return to Egypt'"* (Exodus 13:17-18). I like to think that my small progress over the years was in accordance with God's plan so that I would not be overcome, give up, and want to return to my spiritual Egypt.

SATAN'S OPPOSITION

Satan employs many tactics to cause believers to abandon their God-given destiny. Doubt is one that I particularly have struggled with. In my opinion, the devil has become very adept at using a strategy known as "gaslighting" to seed doubt. It's a tactic that can go unnoticed if you're not intentional about identifying it. It affected my thinking and made me doubt whether what I believed was true.

According to the Psychology Today website, the term "gaslighting" originated from a 1938 play, *Gas Light*, and its film adaptation. The website defines gaslighting as "an insidious form of manipulation and psychological control. Victims of gaslighting are deliberately and systematically fed false information that leads them to question what they know to be true, often about themselves. They may end up doubting their memory, their perception, and even their sanity. Over time, a gaslighter's manipulations can grow more complex and potent, making it increasingly difficult for the victim to see the truth."[20] Since John 10:10 tells us that the devil comes only to steal, kill, and destroy, this tactic is one that all believers need to guard against at all times.

---

19   "Eleven Ways to Renew the Mind," Anna Donahue Ministries, accessed June 2022, https://annadonahueministries.com/free-downloads/.

20   "Gaslighting," Psychology Today, accessed December 2, 2022, https://www.psychologytoday.com/us/basics/gaslighting.

Discouragement, Fear, Frustration, and Accusations

The Books of Ezra and Nehemiah provide additional examples of the devil's attempts to stop believers from fulfilling their purpose. In Ezra, King Cyrus granted the Israelites permission to return to Jerusalem from their exile in Babylon so they could rebuild the Lord's temple. When they arrived, they rebuilt the altar of the Lord *"despite their fear of the peoples around them"* (Ezra 3:3). When these people heard the exiles were allowed to rebuild a temple for the Lord, they set out to discourage them and *"make them afraid to go on building. They hired counselors to work against them and frustrate their plans during the entire reign of Cyrus king of Persia and on to the reign of Darius king of Persia"* (Ezra 4:1-5). Later, during the reign of Kings Xerxes and Artaxerxes, their enemies *"lodged an accusation against the people of Judah and Jerusalem"* and wrote a letter to King Artaxerxes accusing Jerusalem of being a place of revolt against kings and a place of rebellion and sedition (Ezra 4:6-23).

Mocking, Ridicule, and Insults

In the Book of Nehemiah, the Israelites' enemies tried to prevent Nehemiah from rebuilding the wall around Jerusalem. Nehemiah was the cupbearer to King Artaxerxes I, king of Babylon. When the king learned of Nehemiah's sadness over the state of Jerusalem, he granted Nehemiah permission to return and rebuild the wall. He sent Nehemiah on his way with letters to present to the governors of the Trans-Euphrates region and the keeper of the king's forest, ensuring Nehemiah's safe passage, as well as provision of food, drink, and timber for the project. (Nehemiah 2:1-9)

When the Trans-Euphrates officials heard that Nehemiah had come to promote the welfare of the Israelites and to rebuild the wall and gates of Jerusalem, they mocked and ridiculed the Jews. *"What is this you are doing?"* they asked. *"Are you rebelling against the king?"* (Nehemiah 2:19). Nehemiah answered them by saying, *"The God of heaven will give us success* [in rebuilding]," but also assured them that they would have *"no share in Jerusalem or any claim or historic right to it"* (Nehemiah 2:20).

When the officials heard that the Israelites had begun rebuilding the wall, they again ridiculed the Jews in the presence of their associates and the army of Samaria: *"What are those feeble Jews doing?"* they said. *"Will they restore their wall? Will they offer sacrifices? Will they finish in a day? Can they bring the stones back to life from those heaps of rubble—burned as they are?"* (Nehemiah 4:1-2). But Nehemiah prayed that God would turn their insults back onto their own heads and continued rebuilding the wall (Nehemiah 4:4-6).

Threats of Attack and Harm

As the Israelites continued to rebuild, the officials heard that the work was progressing and gaps were being repaired. This infuriated them, and they plotted to cause trouble and fight against the Jews. So, Nehemiah prayed and posted guards day and night to confront the threat. The Jews also learned that their enemies had threatened to sneak up and attack them to stop the work. Nehemiah stationed some of the Jews by families at the weakest points in the wall, equipped them with swords, spears, and bows, and encouraged them to remember the Lord and to fight for their families and homes. When their enemies became aware that their plot had been exposed and that God had frustrated it, the Israelites each returned to their work on the wall. (Nehemiah 4:7-15)

From that day on, Nehemiah instructed half of the men to do the work while the other half stationed themselves behind those building the wall, armed with spears, shields, bows, and armor. Each builder wore a sword at their side, and those transporting materials carried a weapon in one hand. They continued working, using a trumpet to summon help from one another when needed and stayed in the city to serve as guards at night and workmen during the day. They never took off their clothes and always carried a weapon, even when they went for water. (Nehemiah 4:16-23)

When the officials learned that the wall had been rebuilt with no gaps remaining, except for the doors to the gates, they tried once again to stop the work. They invited Nehemiah to meet with them in a village outside the city. Recognizing it was a trap meant to harm him, Nehemiah replied, *"I am carrying on a great project and cannot go down. Why should the work stop while I leave it and go down to you?"* (Nehemiah 6:3). They repeated this message five more times, and on the fifth attempt, they sent a letter accusing the Jews of plotting a revolt and intending to make Nehemiah king. Nehemiah dismissed these claims, saying he had no intention of becoming king and that the officials were imagining things. He understood they were trying to scare the Jews into giving up, believing their strength would weaken and they would be unable to finish the work. So, Nehemiah prayed that God would strengthen his hands. (Nehemiah 6:1-9)

False Prophecies and Intimidation

In their next attempt to undermine Nehemiah, the officials hired a man who falsely claimed to Nehemiah that men were planning to kill him and that he should seek refuge in the temple to save his life. But Nehemiah recognized it as a false prophecy meant to intimidate him. As a layman, Nehemiah was not permitted to enter the sanctuary; the officials aimed to tempt him to sin to discredit his leadership. (Nehemiah 6:10-14)

When the wall was finished and the Jews' enemies learned of it, all the neighboring nations became afraid, recognizing that their God had helped them complete the wall (Nehemiah 6:15-16).

Like Nehemiah, the trials and tribulations we face as we rebuild our living temples will not be in vain. The Lord will use every experience for our good (Romans 8:28). The traumas I experienced in my life and the lessons I learned from those events all have worked together to give me the experience, strength, and hope that I can share with others facing difficult situations. I now know that I am exactly who I am supposed to be, and I am exactly where I am supposed to be in my life. I'm in no way perfect; I'm still in the process of growing and learning. But I realize that nothing in my life has been a mistake. God has used and will continue to use it all for His glory and His purpose.

The Pattern

CONTENDING FOR OUR FAITH

The Israelites were mandated to defeat and eliminate any enemies they encountered in the Promised Land. The Bible states that God left these enemies there so the Israelites wouldn't forget how to fight and to test their obedience to the Lord's commands.

As we pursue becoming all the Lord has called us to be, we likely will face opposition along the way. Every challenge we encounter will transform us into who Christ wants us to become. In the end, everything we experience will be used for good and will provide the experience, strength, and hope necessary to help those in similar situations.

CHAPTER 10
Possessing the Land

Trust in the LORD and do good. Then you will live safely in the land
and prosper. Take delight in the LORD, and he will give you your
heart's desires.

PSALM 37:3-4 (NLT)

My life certainly has been an unexpected journey, full of challenges. As a young girl, I dreamed of having a loving family, a husband who loved me, at least two children—possibly a boy and a girl—and a modest home with a white picket fence. I also wanted to be a teacher. Those were my dreams, but God had other plans. When He entered my life, everything changed. I never sought a life devoted to God. I never even knew if God truly existed. But I knew I had to follow Him once He revealed Himself to me. The Bible says that eternal life is knowing God and His Son, Jesus Christ (John 17:3). When I read that, I knew I wanted that life, because the one I had was miserable, painful, and unfulfilling.

As I grew closer to God through His Word and the experiences He provided, I began to understand more about biblical truth. Jesus teaches us that if we remain faithful to His Word, we will know the truth, and the truth will set us free (John 8:31-32). I believe this truth enables us to live free from sin and worldly corruption, which ultimately leads to death. God desires all people to come to the saving knowledge of the truth and be reconciled to Him through the precious blood of His Son, Jesus Christ (1 Timothy 2:4-6). He wants us to know His love (1 John 4:16) and to experience His righteousness, peace, and joy in the Holy Spirit (Romans 14:17).

TWO KINGDOMS

In this present age, two kingdoms exist: one is visible and one invisible; one is temporary and one eternal. The temporary one is the kingdom of this world. It is a kingdom of darkness, ruled by the god of this world known as Satan, the devil (Luke 4:5-6; Ephesians 2:2). Satan is a fallen angel who was cast out of heaven, along with an unknown number of angels who followed him, and is at enmity and war with the eternal kingdom: God's Kingdom (Revelation 12:7-9, 17; Luke 10:18-19). God's Kingdom is a kingdom of light, ruled by His Son, Jesus Christ (Matthew 28:18, 1 Peter 2:9-10, Ephesians 1:19-23).

All men and women are born through natural childbirth into the kingdom of this world and are under the influence of Satan as a result of original sin committed by Adam and Eve, the first man and woman that God created (Genesis 3:1-7, Romans 5:12). The Bible tells us that sin separates us from a holy God (Isaiah 59:2) and that *"all have sinned and fall short of the glory of God"* (Romans 3:23).

Moreover, the Bible says that the result of sin is death: *"For the wages of sin is death, but the gift of God is eternal life in Christ Jesus our Lord"* (Romans 6:23). A person remains under the influence of Satan unless and until they believe the message that Jesus died on the cross for the forgiveness of their sins, they repent of their sins and accept Jesus Christ as their Lord and Savior, and they surrender their lives to Him (Romans 10:9-10, John 3:5, Acts 2:38).[21]

Under God's original covenant with the Jewish people, priests had to atone for the people's sins by sacrificing a perfect, spotless animal—such as a lamb, bull, or goat—and sprinkling its blood on the altar. God's law states, *"it is the blood that makes atonement for one's life"* (Leviticus 17:11) and *"without the shedding of blood there is no forgiveness* [of sin]" (Hebrews 9:22).

However, Jesus Christ established a new and better covenant for mankind by sacrificing His body and shedding His blood for the forgiveness of our sins. Jesus, God's only Son, was sent to Earth *"in the likeness of sinful man to be a sin offering"* (Romans 8:3). He was the perfect sacrificial Lamb—*"a lamb without blemish or defect"* (1 Peter 1:19)—and God accepted His sacrifice as an atonement for the sins of all those who would believe in Him (John 3:16, 1 John 4:14).

---

21   Romans 10:9-10 tells us, *"That If you confess with your mouth, 'Jesus is Lord,' and believe in your heart that God raised him from the dead, you will be saved. For it is with your heart that you believe and are justified, and it is with your mouth that you confess and are saved."* John 3:5 says that *"no one can enter the kingdom of God unless he is born of water and the Spirit."* Acts 2:38 says, *"Repent and be baptized, every one of you, in the name of Jesus Christ for the forgiveness of your sins. And you will receive the gift of the Holy Spirit."*

Jesus performed many miracles and healed many people during His time on Earth. Even though He was innocent of all crimes, He was arrested by the chief priests and elders of the Jewish people, accused of blasphemy, and sentenced to death (Matthew 26:47-67, John 18). They turned Him over to the Roman governor, and He was severely beaten with a leaded whip until His back was ripped open (John 19:1 TLB).[22]

The soldiers holding Him *"stripped him and put a scarlet robe on him, and then twisted together a crown of thorns and set it on his head"* (Matthew 27:28-29). Then they mocked Him, spat on Him, and struck Him on the head repeatedly (Matthew 27:30). Afterwards, He was led away to be crucified with nails driven into His hands and feet (Matthew 27:31, John 20:25).[23] He hung that way for three hours before crying out in a loud voice and giving up His Spirit (Matthew 27:45-50).

The prophet Isaiah described Jesus' sacrifice this way:

Surely he took up our infirmities and carried our sorrows, yet we considered him stricken by God, smitten by him, and afflicted. But he was pierced for our transgressions, he was crushed for our iniquities; the punishment that brought us peace was upon him, and by his wounds we are healed. We all, like sheep, have gone astray, each of us has turned to his own way; and the LORD has laid on him the iniquity of us all.

He was oppressed and afflicted, yet he did not open his mouth; he was led like a lamb to the slaughter, and as a sheep before her shearers is silent, so he did not open his mouth. By oppression and judgment he was taken away. And who can speak of his descendants? For he was cut off from the land of the living; for the transgression of my people he was stricken. He was assigned a grave with the wicked, and with the rich in his death, though he had done no violence, nor was any deceit in his mouth.

ISAIAH 53:4-9

Three days after Jesus' death on the cross, He was raised to life again! A few of His disciples visited the tomb and discovered that the large stone covering the entrance

---

22 The King James Version (KJV) states that *"Pilate took Jesus and scourged him."* A commentary on this verse states that "Jesus was **scourged** according to Roman practice. The blows came from a whip with many leather strands, each having sharp pieces of bone or metal at the ends. It reduced the back to raw flesh, and it was not unusual for a criminal to die from a scourging, even before crucifixion." (Guzik, D., "Study Guide for John 19 by David Guzik," Blue Letter Bible, last modified 6/2022, https:// www.blueletterbible.org/comm/guzik_david/study-guide/john/john-19.cfm.)

23 *The NIV Study Bible* notes that crucifixion was a "Roman means of execution in which the victim was nailed to a cross. Heavy, wrought-iron nails were driven through the wrists and the heel bones. If the life of the victim lingered too long, death was hastened by breaking his legs." (See note on Mark 15:24 in Zondervan Corporation, *The NIV Study Bible*, 10th Anniversary ed. [Grand Rapids, MI: Zondervan Publishing House, 1995], 1526.)

had been rolled away, and the tomb was empty. An angel appeared and told them that Jesus was not there; He had risen! (Matthew 27:57–28:15)[24]

Later, Jesus appeared to His eleven remaining disciples[25] and to more than five hundred believers at the same time, as well as others (1 Corinthians 15:6). Then, He was taken up to Heaven (Luke 24:50-53) and seated at the right hand of the Father *"in the heavenly realms, far above all rule and authority, power and dominion, and every title that can be given, not only in the present age but also in the one to come"* (Ephesians 1:20-21).

LOVED, CHOSEN, AND SET APART

Just as Jesus was raised to life and seated with the Father, every person who believes in Him also is raised to life and seated with Him in the heavenly realms (Ephesians 2:6). Every believer crosses over from death to life (John 5:24) and is reconciled to God through the shed blood of Jesus Christ (Colossians 1:19-20). Colossians 1:12-14 tells us that *"the Father…has qualified you* [the believer] *to share in the inheritance of the saints in the kingdom of light. For he has rescued us from the dominion of darkness and brought us into the kingdom of the Son he loves, in whom we have redemption, the forgiveness of sins."*

The believer becomes a new creation in Christ, a co-heir with Christ, and an ambassador for Christ on Earth (2 Corinthians 5:17, 20; Romans 8:17). This new position in Christ exists by grace alone because of the believer's faith in Jesus, and it is sealed with the Holy Spirit (Ephesians 2:8-9, 1:13-14).

As a new creation in Christ, every believer is loved and chosen (Ephesians 1:4-5). Just as God formed us in our mothers' wombs (Jeremiah 1:5, Psalm 139:13-16), He will transform us into the new person He intends for us to be. He has a plan to prosper us and to see that His plan is fulfilled. Everything we need to accomplish God's purpose in our lives already has been provided for us (2 Peter 1:3), and God will prepare us to step into that purpose. His Word says, *"'For I know the plans I have for you,' declares the LORD, 'plans to prosper you and not to harm you, plans to give you hope and a future'"* (Jeremiah 29:11). Philippians 1:6 says, *"…being confident of this, that he who began a good work in you will carry it on to completion until the day of Christ Jesus."*

---

24   See also Mark 15:42–16:14, Luke 23:50–24:49, and John 19:38–20:31.

25   Jesus originally had twelve disciples, but one of them—Judas Iscariot—betrayed Jesus to the Jewish leaders for 30 pieces of silver. When Judas saw that Jesus had been condemned to death, he became filled with remorse, threw the money into the temple, and *"went away and hanged himself"* (Matthew 27:1-5).

To prepare us for our purpose, however, God first must mold and shape us to become more like His Son. Before becoming believers, we were molded and shaped by the world. Just as a potter molds and shapes clay into the vessel he wants to use, God does the same with us to become the vessels He desires (Jeremiah 18:1-6). This process of sanctification includes purifying our hearts, minds, and bodies to become more like Christ. 1 Peter 1:15-16 tells us, *"But just as he who called you is holy, so be holy in all you do; for it is written: 'Be holy, because I am holy.'"* Also, 1 John 3:2-3 says, *"But we know that when he appears, we shall be like him, for we shall see him as he is. Everyone who has this hope in him purifies himself, just as he is pure."*[26]

The Bible makes it clear that sanctification is God's will for us (1 Thessalonians 4:3, 5:23; 2 Thessalonians 2:13; and 2 Timothy 2:21). Sanctification may include times of persecution, trials, and testing. It also may require us to renew our minds, give up bad habits, or surrender our own agendas. God may even ask us to let go of everything we want to achieve in order to serve Him, but the good news is that we will discover what we were made for when we do! Matthew 10:39 promises that we will find happiness living the specific purpose for which God created us: *"Whoever finds his life will lose it, and whoever loses his life for my sake will find it."* In addition, James 1:12 says, *"Blessed is the man who perseveres under trial, because when he has stood the test, he will receive the crown of life that God has promised to those who love him."*

The Kingdom Is the Promise

My pastor once preached a message about living on the land and referenced Psalm 37:3-4 (NLT), which says, *"Trust in the LORD and do good. Then you will live safely in the land and prosper."* He explained that when people live on the land, they have everything they need to live successfully, accomplish what they need to accomplish, be safe and happy, and have all their needs met—no wants, no lack, no fear. It's the same for us, he said. It may be hard work, but it's worth it.[27]

In the Old Testament, God promised Moses—God's chosen leader of the Jews— that He would deliver the Israelites from Egyptian oppression and bring them into *"a good and spacious land, a land flowing with milk and honey"* (Exodus 3:7-8).[28] Additionally, God renewed a covenant with Moses that He had made with Moses'

---

26   Also see Romans 8:29, 2 Corinthians 3:18, and Ephesians 4:1.
27   Rev. Bryan A. Tomes, Crossroads Community Church, https://crossroadsconnects.com.
28   See also Leviticus 20:24, Numbers 14:8, Joshua 1:13, Ezekiel 20:15, and more in the Old Testament.

forefathers—Abraham, Isaac, and Jacob (Exodus 19:3-6, 2:24). With each of these covenants, God promised them land (Exodus 6:3-8).[29] This land, where God promised to dwell with His people,[30] is described in Hebrews 11:9 as the "promised land:" *"By faith he* [Abraham] *made his home in the promised land like a stranger in a foreign country; he lived in tents, as did Isaac and Jacob, who were heirs with him of the same promise."*

Psalm 37 (NIV) describes some of the blessings that await those who inherit this land *"flowing with milk and honey":*

- They will *"dwell in the land and enjoy safe pasture"* (v. 3).
- The Lord will give them the desires of their hearts (v. 4).
- He will make their reward *"shine like the dawn"* and their *"vindication like the noonday sun"* (v. 6).
- Evildoers *"will be destroyed"* (v. 9).
- They will *"enjoy peace and prosperity"* (v. 11).
- The *"power of the wicked will be broken"* (v. 17).
- Their *"inheritance will endure forever"* (v. 18).
- They will not wither *"in times of disaster"* and *"will enjoy plenty"* in days of famine (v. 19).
- Their enemies *"will be consumed"* (v. 20).
- They will *"give generously"* (v. 21).
- They will be blessed and *"inherit the land"* (v. 22).
- They may stumble, but will not fall (v. 24).
- *"They are always generous and lend freely; their children will be a blessing"* (v. 26).
- They will not be forsaken (v. 28).
- They will *"inherit the land and dwell in it forever"* (v. 29).
- They will speak wisdom and *"what is just"* (v. 30).
- God's law will be in their hearts and their feet will not slip (v. 31).
- They will not be left *"in the power of the wicked"* or *"condemned when brought to trial"* (v. 33).
- They will be exalted *"to inherit the land"* and will see the wicked destroyed (v 34).
- A future awaits them (v. 37).
- The Lord will help them, deliver them from the wicked, and save them (v. 40).

---

29 Jonathan Shuttlesworth – Adalis Shuttlesworth, "#SpiteAThon2023: MILLION DOLLAR MIRACLE NIGHT with Rodney Howard Browne!" *Facebook*, March 31, 2023, https://www.facebook. com/RevivalToday/videos/spiteathon2023-million-dollar-miracle-night-with-rodney-howard-browne/1418949308919100. See also Genesis 13:14-15; 15:18-21; 17:2, 4-8; 26:2-3; and 28:13-15.

30 Chris Bruno, Ph.D., "Why Does the Bible Talk So Much About Land?" May 5, 2017, https://www. crossway.org/articles/why-does-the-bible-talk-so-much-about-land. See also Exodus 29:45.

God's promise of this inheritance came with a qualification, however. The Israelites had to obey the Lord and separate themselves from the surrounding nations:

Keep all my decrees and laws and follow them, so that the land where I am bringing you to live may not vomit you out. You must not live according to the customs of the nations I am going to drive out before you. Because they did all these things, I abhorred them. But I said to you, 'You will possess their land; I will give it to you as an inheritance, a land flowing with milk and honey.' I am the LORD your God, who has set you apart from the nations.

LEVITICUS 20:22-24

Under the new and better covenant established through Jesus' sacrifice, the Bible tells us that Jesus is our mediator—the go-between or the intermediary—between God the Father and humankind. Those who believe in Him will receive a promised eternal inheritance that He died to give us (Hebrews 9:15).[31]

The Bible also states that we are God's children and co-heirs with Christ (Romans 8:16-17). Galatians 3:29 says that we are *"Abraham's seed, and heirs according to the promise."* In Luke 17:21, Jesus tells us that *"the kingdom of God is within you,"* or *"in your midst,"* or *"already among you,"* as different versions have translated it. Finally, James 2:5 tells us that those who love God will inherit the kingdom that He promised.

When you consider all of these statements—we have a covenant with God the Father through Christ, we are God's children and co-heirs with Christ, we are Abraham's seed and heirs of the promise, the kingdom dwells within us, those who love God will inherit the promised kingdom, and the promise is an eternal inheritance that includes land—it illustrates that our Promised Land is a metaphor for the Kingdom of God.[32]

Therefore, the Kingdom is the promise![33]

I believe that our Promised Land—or the land of God's promises—is the Kingdom of God within us and in our lives. It represents an eternal, spiritual place where we have all provision and protection to live safely and prosper in this life, as well as in the one to come, as described in Psalm 37. It is a place where we dwell as God's covenant people—both in this world and in the heavenly realms—a place of peace, provision,

---

31   See also Hebrews 7:22, 8:6-13 and 12:24.

32   Although this was a personal revelation given to me by the Holy Spirit, Luke 12:32 specifically states, *"Do not be afraid little flock, for your Father has been pleased to give you the kingdom."* Other authors have written about this also. See the following in the list of References: (1) Staff, "Thy Kingdom Come! (Part One), in *Forerunner*, "Prophecy Watch;" (2) Matthew Tuininga, "The Two Kingdoms Doctrine, Part Three: The Teaching of Scripture;" and (3) "two kingdoms," jesus loves : the world.

33   See also Luke 17:20-21.

protection, prosperity, and purpose representing the resurrected, abundant life that Jesus died for (Ephesians 2:6; John 10:10 ESV). It is a place where we possess spiritual power, dominion, and authority over the enemy of our souls (Luke 10:19). Above all, it is a place where we can experience restored communion with God, the Father, and His Son, Jesus Christ, through His Spirit, His Word, and the fellowship of believers (Matthew 28:20, Hebrews 13:5).

Our Promised Land is God's Kingdom. We carry it within us, we represent it on this Earth, and we dwell in it spiritually.

Never forget, however, that we have an enemy who is at enmity with God. John 10:10 (ESV) says, "*The thief comes only to steal and kill and destroy.*" Our enemy wants people to believe they can make their own way in the world and that they don't need God. That is a lie! We need God, and we have a choice: we can live in the kingdom of darkness that leads to death—the world—or we can live in the Kingdom of light that leads to an abundant life—God's Kingdom.

HOW LONG WILL YOU WAIT?

My goal in writing this book was to illustrate, through the recounting of the Israelites' journey to the Promised Land and my own experiences, that the Old Testament reveals a recurring pattern of how God delivers His people from bondage to the kingdom of darkness and restores them to His Kingdom of light through His Son, Jesus Christ. I hope I have achieved this. I further hope that if believers recognize this is the pattern of God's deliverance and restoration of His people, they will not be discouraged and abandon their faith during times of testing. Instead, I hope they will persevere in their faith and allow God to mature them until they reach the Promised Land in their lives.

It's important to note that, when warning about the disobedience and evil practices of the Israelites that caused many to die in the wilderness, the Apostle Paul wrote, "*These things happened to them as examples and were written down as warnings for us, on whom the culmination of the ages has come*" (1 Corinthians 10:11 NIV).

Joshua asked the Israelites, "*How long will you wait before you begin to take possession of the land that the LORD, the God of your fathers, has given you?*" (Joshua 18:3). I'll ask you the same question: how long will you wait to take possession of the land that the Lord has given you? Are you ready to kill the giants in your life and inherit the Kingdom?

"Do not fear; only believe," Jesus said in Mark 5:36 (ESV). I echo Jesus' exhortation: "Only believe!" Let your heart and mind be changed and begin to walk in God's redemptive path to your Promised Land.

You can begin that walk right now, or renew it, by inviting Jesus into your life and saying the following prayer aloud and truly mean it from your heart (Romans 10:9-10):

Prayer of Salvation[34]

"Heavenly Father, I come to You admitting that I am a sinner. Right now, I choose to turn away from sin, and I ask you to cleanse me of all unrighteousness. I believe that Your Son, Jesus, died on the cross to take away my sins. I also believe that He rose again from the dead so that I might be forgiven of my sins and made righteous through faith in Him. I call upon the name of Jesus Christ to be the Savior and Lord of my life. Jesus, I choose to follow You and ask that You fill me with the power of the Holy Spirit. I declare that right now I am a child of God. I am free from sin and full of the righteousness of God. I am saved in Jesus' name. Amen."

If you prayed the above prayer of salvation, I encourage you to find a good Christian church to attend that will guide you in your walk with the Lord (Acts 2:42-47, Hebrews 10:24-25). I also encourage you to commit to reading and studying the Bible regularly so you will learn more about who God is, who you are in Christ, and the devil's schemes to derail you (2 Timothy 3:16-17). Finally, I encourage you to get water baptized, which symbolizes your death and resurrection with Jesus (Acts 2:38), and to follow and obey the leading of the Holy Spirit (Romans 8:14-16).

---

34   Taken from T. L. Osborn, D.D., D.H.L., "Prayer of Salvation," in *Healing the Sick* (Tulsa, Oklahoma: Harrison House Publishers, 1951, 1977, 1981, 1986, 1992) 367.

References

Anna Donahue Ministries. "Eleven Ways to Renew the Mind." Accessed June 2022. https://annadonahueministries.com/free-downloads/.

Baker, John. *Celebrate Recovery Leader's Guide.* Grand Rapids, Michigan: Zondervan, 1998, 2005.

Bible Gateway. *Holy Bible, New International Version*®, (NIV®). Biblica, Inc.®, 1973, 1978, 1984, 2011. Accessed June 18, 2023. https://www.biblegateway.com/passage/?search=psalm+37&version=NIV.

Bible Gateway. *Holy Bible, New Living Translation* (NLT). Tyndale House Foundation, 1996, 2004, 2015. Accessed June 18, 2023. https://www.biblegateway.com/passage/?search=Psalm+37%3A3-4&version=NLT.

Bible Gateway. *New American Standard Bible*® (NASB). The Lockman Foundation, 1960, 1971, 1977, 1995, 2020. lockman.org. Accessed May 15, 2023. https://www.biblegateway.com/passage/?search=2+Corinthians+3%3A18&version=NASB.

Bible Gateway. *New King James Version*® (NKJV). Thomas Nelson, 1982. Accessed May 15, 2023. https://www.biblegateway.com/passage/?search=Proverbs+23%3A7&version=NKJV.

Bible Gateway. *The Holy Bible, English Standard Version*, (ESV®). Text Edition: 2016. Crossway Bibles, 2001. Accessed June 18, 2023. https://www.biblegateway.com/passage/?search=John+10%3A10&version=ESV.

Bible Gateway. *The Living Bible* (TLB). Tyndale House Foundation, 1971. Accessed June 18, 2023. https://www.biblegateway.com/passage/?search=John+19%3A1-3&version=TLB.

Bonding Psychotherapy. "What is Bonding Psychotherapy." Accessed July 4, 2020. https://www.bonding-psychotherapy.org/about/what-is-bonding-psychotherapy.

Bruno, Chris, Ph.D. "Why Does the Bible Talk So Much About Land?" May 5, 2017. https://www.crossway.org/articles/why-does-the-bible-talk-so-much-about-land.

Casriel, Daniel, M.D. *A Scream Away from Happiness*. New York: Grosset & Dunlap, 1972.

Celebrate Recovery. "About Us: Our History." Accessed August 13, 2024. https://celebraterecovery.com/about.

Dyer, Douglas, Jr., Pastor. *Facebook*. January 11, 2021. https://www.facebook.com.

Guzik, David, "Study Guide for John 19 by David Guzik," Blue Letter Bible, last modified 6/2022, https://www.blueletterbible.org/comm/guzik_david/study-guide/john/john-19.cfm.

jesus loves : the world. "two kingdoms." Accessed October 19, 2023. https://jesuslovestheworld.info/sermon/battle-of-two-kingdoms.

Kenneth Copeland Ministries. "What Does It Mean to 'Renew My Mind'?" Accessed September 19, 2025. https://www.kcm.org/real-help/spiritual-growth/apply/what-does-it-mean-renew-my-mind?language_content_entity=en-US.

Mahoney, James. *Journey into Fullness: From Bondage to Conquest in the Christian Life*. Nashville, Tennessee: Broadman Press, 1974.

Meyer, Joyce. *Battlefield of the Mind*. Faith Words ed. New York: Hachette Book Group USA, 2002.

Osborn, T. L., D.D., D.H.L., "Prayer of Salvation." In *Healing the Sick*. Tulsa, Oklahoma: Harrison House Publishers, 1951, 1977, 1981, 1986, 1992.

Psychology Today. "Gaslighting." Accessed December 2, 2022. https://www.psychologytoday.com/us/basics/gaslighting.

Shuttlesworth, Jonathan – Adalis. "#SpiteAThon2023: MILLION DOLLAR MIRACLE NIGHT with Rodney Howard Browne!" *Facebook*. March 31, 2023. https://www.facebook.com/RevivalToday/videos/spiteathon2023-million-dollar-miracle-night-with-rodney-howard-browne/1418949308919100.

Staff. "Thy Kingdom Come! (Part One)." In *Forerunner*, "Prophecy Watch," July-August 2010. Bible Tools. Accessed October 19, 2023. https://www.bibletools.org/index.cfm/fuseaction/Library.sr/CT/PW/k/1495/thy-kingdom-come-part-one.htm.

Tomes, Bryan A., Rev. Crossroads Community Church. https://crossroadsconnects.com.

Tuininga, Matthew. "The Two Kingdoms Doctrine, Part Three: The Teaching of Scripture." Reformation21. November 19, 2012. https://www. reformation21.org/featured/the-two-kingdoms-doctrine-part-three-the-teaching-of-scripture.php.

Wikipedia contributors. "Daniel Harold Casriel." Wikipedia, The Free Encyclopedia. Accessed July 4, 2020, https://en.wikipedia.org/wiki/Daniel_Harold_Casriel.

Wikipedia contributors. "Pandora's box." Wikipedia, The Free Encyclopedia. Accessed April 18, 2024. https://en.wikipedia.org/wiki/Pandora%27s_box.

Wikipedia contributors. "Synanon." Wikipedia, The Free Encyclopedia. Accessed July 4, 2020. https://en.wikipedia.org/wiki/Synanon.

Zondervan Corporation. *The NIV Study Bible*, 10th Anniversary ed. Grand Rapids, MI: Zondervan Publishing House, 1995.

About the Author

Harriet Allen is a retired communications professional and former educator with over 40 years' experience in writing, editing, publishing, and education. She has worked as a technical writer and proposal specialist for various government contractors, managed a professional journal in optometric education, and taught 7th and 8th grade language arts.

Harriet is a grateful believer in Jesus Christ who has overcome depression, codependency, fear, love addiction, being an adult child of an alcoholic, and childhood abuse. She loves to share her experience, strength, and hope to help others and to see them set free from hurts, hang-ups, and habits that keep them from becoming all that they can be in Christ Jesus.

Harriet resides outside the greater Boston area. She is active within her local church and enjoys spending time with her children and four grandchildren. You can contact Harriet at HarrietAllen.author@outlook.com.